THE B.

their struggle f

THE BASQUES

their struggle for independence

Luis Núñez Astrain

translated from the French by
Meic Stephens

with an introduction by Ned Thomas

Welsh Academic Press

Published in Wales by Welsh Academic Press 1997

Welsh Academic Press is an imprint of
Ashley Drake Publishing Ltd

ISBN   186057 0186

British Library Cataloguing-in-Publication Data.
A catalogue record for this book is available from the
British Library.

Typeset by Westkey Ltd, Falmouth, Cornwall
Printed and bound in Wales By
Creative Print & Design (Wales), Ebbw Vale

CONTENTS

PREFACE

Ned Thomas

The political situation of the Basque people, like every other situation, is unique. We can only begin to make judgements when we understand its complexity, which this book will help us to do. But the Basques also raise in an acute form and close to home the issue of self-determination which is of world-wide relevance – whether in East Timor or Chechnya or Kurdistan. Can there be democracy without the right of self-determination or when the electoral and administrative boundaries make self-determination impossible?

For us in Wales, the Basques offer some instructive parallels and contrasts. The Basque language, like the Welsh language, is a central feature of identity, and the linguistic demography is quite similar. Moreover the culture is both rural and old heavy-industrial. In the fields of education, public administration and the media, linguistic policy and practice, a lot is going on in the Spanish Basque country today which we can learn from.

But that all sounds rather general, and what I have to say here is more personal. Though I have come to know quite a lot about the Basques over the years it is not as an expert that I write now but rather as one who has made friends of individual Basques and also observed and been moved by their communal life, not only in its dramatic moments but in the daily struggle and commitment of extraordinary ordinary people.

I passed through the Basque country a dozen times during the early 1960s when I taught at the University of Salamanca. Even by the standards of Franco's Spain the industrial towns of the Spanish Basque country seemed grey, sullen and neglected. Any protest was blacked out in the Spanish media and there was no public presence whatever of Euskera, the Basque language, nor do I remember once hearing it spoken. Yet there was a whole world there waiting to surface.

I was introduced to that world in the early 1970s. A Basque in France – a political refugee from the Spanish Basque country – read my book *The Welsh Extremist* and wrote to me. I subsequently visited him just north of the Franco-Spanish border and was introduced to a number of people active in Basque movements. In particular I remember Telesforo Monzon, the last surviving minister of the Basque government which came into existence during the Spanish Civil War. He was an old man, close on seven foot tall and straight as a ramrod. He had led a lengthy hunger-strike in Bayonne Cathedral against French Government policy towards Basque refugees.

From him and from my friends I learnt of the deep sense of betrayal felt by the Basques at the end of the Second World War. Here was a people whose anti-fascist credentials were impeccable. The bombing of Gernika was not just another episode in the Civil War, it was directed at the traditional capital of the Basques who were resisting as a people. Even the Church in the Basque country had sided with the people against the generals. Alone among the bishops in Spain, the Bishop of Gasteiz (Vitoria) asked the Pope (in vain) not to give his blessing to one side in the war in Spain.

When that war was lost thousands left the Basque Country. Wales took in many children. Others went to the Soviet Union. Large numbers of Basques crossed into France and played a prominent part in the *Maquis*. At the end of the Second World War De Gaulle addressed the Basque Batallion in Bordeaux (I have read the news-paper cuttings) promising that the allies would not stop at the Pyrenees but destroy fascism wherever it was found.

This did not happen. There was a half-hearted economic boycott of Spain in the immediate post-war years, but Franco played the anti-Communist card and before long the USA was paying to place a nuclear submarine base at Rota in the south of Spain, and the French were selling Mirage jets to Franco. He made one small condition – the removal from the French side of the border of listed Basque nationalists. 'At least I know now I am worth three Mirages', Telesforo Monzon told me.

It was in the early 1950s that a young generation arose in the Basque country that realized it could not expect salvation from without, but must do things for itself. This generation set about economic regeneration through the now famous Mondragón co-operatives; it established the *ikastola* (Basque schools) movement; and it set up a cultural and language movement, EKIN, later to become ETA. It was a heroic generation, operating in clandestine conditions initially, subject to persecution and torture and exile in France without social security rights. It drew its strength from the tremendous communal consciousness of the Basque people which was no doubt cemented by the years of Franco oppression but is not wholly explained by that.

In the early 1970s (the last years of Franco) I visited the Spanish Basque country several times, with a list of contacts supplied by my friends north of the border. In an industrial valley town I was taken round an *ikastola:* Form 1 was at the back of a baker's shop, Form 2 in a church vestry and so on. No state money supported the system. The parents in the town contributed to the cost of transport for the country children. They were building a brand-new school up above the valley with money that was borrowed from a bank on the security of all the members of the school association. *Batasuna* in Basque means something like 'together' or *gyda'n gilydd*. It was the title of a song which, unsurprisingly, was banned under Franco. It enters into the name of the left-nationalist party *Herri Batasuna*, the people or the country all together.

Out in the mountains of Nafarroa I remember asking the local priest where the linguistic border ran. He explained to me that things didn't work quite like that. His own village spoke Basque because his predecessor had guaranteed the good behaviour of his parishioners when Franco's troops had arrived, and they had not stayed. A village which he pointed to on a hillside a few miles distant had been occupied and there the Basque language had died – more or less overnight at the public level. In 1939 you could be shot for speaking Basque, and even small gatherings of Basques were forbidden. Older people who had little Spanish feared to go out of their houses. After Franco, when *Euskera* was again seen and heard on the streets and the radio, numbers of adults who had been children in the immediate post-war period found they had some small memory of the spoken language. I have even heard of a couple who discovered on Franco's death, after many years of married life, that they could both understand the language.

Then there is the political drama of the streets and public places. In the 1970s and 1980s I can hardly remember a visit to Euskadi in which I did not witness a mass demonstration of some kind, sometimes completely peaceful as when thousands of people run through the streets of Bilbo to raise money for the Basque to Adults programme, sometimes confrontational when the Guardia Civil in Donostia (San Sebastián) would drive out of their fortified stockade near the harbour in armoured Land Rovers and block the path of a march. On the evenings after such events the young people would set tyres burning in the streets of the old town in scenes reminiscent of Belfast. And then there were the general strikes when a whole town,

or the whole country, would come to a standstill to honour an ETA
leader assassinated by GAL or some other shadowy paramilitary
front organization working for the Spanish government. One ETA
leader's ashes were scattered from a boat by his widow into the river
Bidasoa which divides the Spanish and French Basque country.
Despite the best efforts of the police, thousands had turned out.
Whatever one's view of ETA, it was a memorable scene – the woman
in the boat floating slowly downstream, the crowds in completely
silent homage on each bank of the river.

But that, it will be said, was a long time ago, before democracy
came to Spain. Why should the struggle now continue?

This book sets out to answer that question and I shall not repeat
the arguments, except to say this. The situation is now much more
complicated. There is a Basque nationalist government in Euskadi
(the area of three provinces that constitute the official Spanish
Basque country) and there is a Basque nationalist opposition, and
these are not just two political parties but two cultures. One has the
power of patronage, the other inherits the tradition of communal
solidarity and struggle. There is now a Basque police force as well
as several Spanish ones. The Basque police have been accused of
torturing suspects and ETA has shot at least one Basque policeman.
There are now tragic tones and hints of civil war within the Basque
community.

ETA's conditions for peace are the reunification of Nafarroa, (or
at least the Basque areas of Nafarroa) with the autonomous region
of Euskadi, and then a vote by the Basque people on their political
future which includes the option of leaving Spain. This is not possible
within the present Spanish constitution, nor technically is any party
supposed to advocate it.

Most Basques vote for the nationalist parties. Most Basques would
agree with the principles of reunification and self-determination. But
not all Basques support the armed struggle in pursuit of those ends.
But other roads to those ends seem to be blocked by the Spanish
constitution. The army is till a force in Spanish politics as ETA is in
Basque politics; and there is a terrorism of the state as there is of
national resistance. I know this not just from the newspapers but from
the experience of friends. By 1989 the friend who first wrote to me
from the Basque Country, the mathematician, novelist and political
thinker Txillardegi, had been elected a Senator of the Upper House
in the Madrid Parliament on behalf of *Herri Batasuna*. He was dining
there, in the Hotel Alcalá, with six other elected parliamentarians of
his party and three journalists, when masked men burst into the room
and began shooting. One of the group was killed on the spot, another

lingered long in hospital. This can be called state terrorism. It can be called war. What it cannot be called is democracy in action.

Just as the 'Irish Question' is part of the 'British Question', so the 'Basque problem' is part of the 'Spanish problem'. Why should dominant nations be so selectively in favour of self-determination – for it in Lithuania or Slovenia, against it in Chechnya or the Basque Country? These are questions we all need to address if the world is not to be convulsed by an endless series of so-called 'ethnic' conflicts.

INTRODUCTION

What do the Basques want now? Don't they already have a democratic system comparable with that of any other European country?
Don't they enjoy a substantial measure of autonomy? So what is the
point of their interminable protests, their huge demonstrations, their
armed struggle?

Many people in Europe have some knowledge of the Basque
Country because they have heard of the Nazi bombardment which
destroyed the town of Guernica in 1937; or else they have read about
the infamous Burgos Trials of 1970, or perhaps the assassination of
Admiral Carrero Blanco, Franco's right-hand man, in 1973. More
recently, they may have heard of the frequent outbreaks of violence
which have occurred in the Basque Country. But most don't have any
clear idea about what is happening there, nor do they understand the
causes of the conflict between the Basques and the Spanish and
French Governments.

The Basque Country does not really exist as an entity of its own,
with a unity that is generally recognized by others. Its territory on the
northern side of the Franco-Spanish border has been denied even the
smallest degree of autonomy, while on the southern side it is divided
into two distinct parts. Nevertheless, when Sabino Arana, the father
of Basque Nationalism, was still in his cradle, Victor Hugo, who was
well acquainted with the Basque Country, wrote in the first volume
of his novel, *L'homme qui rit* (1869), 'A Basque is neither a Spaniard
nor a Frenchman. He is a Basque.'

In our own day every Basque is called upon to cast his vote on six
separate occasions, but the voter who lives in Saint-Jean-de-Luz will
vote for one set of institutions, the one in San Sebastián for others,
and the one in Pamplona for yet others.

The political institutions of the Basque Country at the present time
are complex and confused, and far from making up an entity peculiar
to the Basques, they have exactly the opposite effect, of actually

preventing the people from achieving unity. It is not that these political institutions do not work but that they exist in excessive numbers. There are too many of them and their functions are too various. What is lacking, in short, are institutions with a unitary function which would make for cohesion and ensure the sovereignty of a country which stands in great need of them. Most Basques consider a greater degree of unity to be essential if they are to maintain the heritage they hold in common, whether it be the culture of the Basque language, consigned to the scrapheap by Spanish and French, or else the country's economic life, which has suffered unprecedented industrial decline with resulting widespread unemployment — especially among the working class.

This book will attempt to explain why the Basque Country has not been officially recognized, why it is politically divided, and why there is discrimination against its language. It will describe the twofold response of the country itself, first of all in the creation of the *Partido Nacionalista Vasco* (The Basque Nationalist Party), and then of *Euskadi Ta Askatasuna*, otherwise known as *ETA*. Other responses which have been made throughout the country's history will also be outlined in Chapter 5.

The reaction of the Spanish and French Governments, which persist in their denial of the Basque identity, has always been one of repression, sometimes going as far as the use of illegal methods. The Franco regime, which lasted from 1939 to 1975, introduced police torture during interrogations and a policy of 'shoot to kill', that is to say, of firing at militant Basques rather than arresting them. The Government of the Spanish Democratic Right (*UCD*, 1976-81) added to these illegal methods the deployment of irregular police units. In addition to all this, the Government of the Spanish Left (*PSOE*, 1982-96) went in for the systematic beating of prisoners.

The illegal methods used to suppress the Basques, usually with help from the French Government, sometimes discreet and sometimes open, depending on the climate of the times, are still being used today. They are the more or less inevitable consequence of a longstanding anti-democratic attitude, namely the negation of the Basque identity, and a very serious denial of the rights which these Governments claim to defend. Without such repression, the Spanish and French Governments would find it impossible to go on denying the Basque people their right to exist. The many civil servants and local officials who commit illicit acts do so with almost total impunity.

This book will also have something to say about the various movements which have long fought for the Basque people's interests in the fields of ecology, public health, education, equality of the sexes and races, and peace, and especially those organizations which have fostered their desire for a more developed, more real sense of democracy than the electoral kind. We shall be particularly concerned with those movements which are in the process of converting the Basque people into pioneers of a new outlook that is now beginning to knock timidly on the doors of Europe, one which strives to endow democracy with the capacity to involve people on an increasing scale. The book will end with a comparison of the Basque and Irish questions and will review the rights of all European peoples to self-determination as this century draws to its close.

What is usually but erroneously called 'the Basque problem' is not in fact a Basque problem, or the problem of the Basques, at all. What the Basques are seeking is nothing more than a minimum of recognition as a nation, their official status as a territorial entity and the normalization of their language. If the problem consists of the threat posed by *ETA* to the Spanish Government, that is a Spanish problem, but it is not 'the Basque problem'.

The two sides of this issue are bound closely together and the resolution of one without the other does not appear to be possible at the present time. Some while ago, on 18 April 1982, just before his party came to power, the leader of the *PSOE*, José Maria Benegas, said with his tongue in cheek, 'For a long time now I've been hearing from Ministers of the Interior that we are witnessing the last twitches of *ETA*.' Today, it is only necessary to add that Ministers of the *PSOE* were themselves content to repeat the same thing when they were in power.

Unfortunately, the Basque cause is as misunderstood by the Spanish Left as it is by the Spanish Right, and that is why this book will be of interest, whatever the Governments of Madrid and Paris may do or say or whichever party is in power. The distinguished Basque Nationalist, the late Telesforo Monzón, a parliamentarian in the time of the Republic but also during the post-Franco period, was fond of saying, 'The Spanish have always sided with the Basques when they found themselves in opposition. But once they come to power, this sympathy always wanes. When the Left was in power, we became troglodytes, dwellers in caves, capitalists, a Vatican in miniature. When the Right was in power, we were Freemasons, Reds, Separatists, people who had sold out to Moscow.'

The aim of this book is therefore to throw light on the Basque national question, and it will make no attempt to go into any of the country's other problems or contradictions, although some reference will have to be made to them from time to time. Its intention is to review the national question from a global point of view, and readers who are already familiar with some aspects of the subject may not need to read it all. Those who have a very good knowledge of the situation of the Basque language, for example, or of the repression which has taken place in the country, or of the historical dimension, may not wish to read this book in its entirety. The chapters which are essential reading for an understanding of the subject are probably the first and the last.

Chapter 1

A COUNTRY WITHOUT A FRAMEWORK

A Basque attaches such importance to his language that he defines himself by his ability to speak it, that is to say, in linguistic terms. He does not refer to himself in terms of race or tribe, or religion, or geographical locality, but exclusively in relationship to his language. In the Basque language, in order to convey that someone is a Basque, one says that he or she is *euskaldun*, which means more precisely 'Basque-speaking' or 'in possession of the Basque language'. Basque has no other way of saying 'a Basque'. We therefore have a problem in knowing how to refer to those who are native to the Basque Country but do not speak its language; this, however, is only a secondary problem. For the moment, the most important thing is to underline the supreme significance which the Basque has traditionally given to his or her language.

Furthermore, the Basque Country defines itself in Basque as *Euskal Herria,* the etymological significance of which is 'the Basque-speaking nation', which refers as much to the country as to the people. Another word denoting the Basque Country or *Euskal Herria,* which has been in use for a century or more, is *Euskadi,* but it has more political connotations.

Struck by the Basques' attachment to their language, which he had observed during his visit to the country, Victor Hugo wrote in his book *Les Pyrénées* (1843), 'The Basque language is the land itself, almost a religion.'

'If the history of the last three thousand years,' concluded the historian Roger Collins in his book *Les Basques,* published by Alianza Editorial in 1989, 'has any lesson to teach us, it is doubtless that the permanence of the Basque identity owes more to linguistic than to political independence.'

'The existence of the Basques today, as a people or community, is essentially due to the survival of the language,' wrote our famous linguist Koldo Mitxelena, who died in 1987. 'It is no accident that the limits of what is known as the Basque Country (however imprecise they may be, according to one's point of view) correspond with the territory of the Basque language, nor that they exclude those regions where the language was lost several centuries ago.'

So the extent of the national language has traditionally coincided with the territory that is usually considered to be Basque. The words *Euskal Herria* are applied today by Basque-speakers to the provinces of Álava (Basque, Araba), Guipúzcoa (Gipuzkoa) and Vizcaya (Biskaia) on the Spanish side; to those of Labourd (Lapurdi) and Soule (Zuberoa) on the French; and to Navarra (Nafarroa), part of which, Basse Navarre (BeNafarroa), is on the French side of the frontier. The Basque Country therefore has, if Navarra is considered as a single entity, six provinces. On the other hand, if Basse Navarre is distinguished from southern Navarra, it has seven, and that is the number commonly referred to ever since the birth of Basque Nationalism at the end of the 19th century. Pamplona, the capital of Navarra, is also the former Basque capital, while Saint-Jean-de-Port is the capital of Basse Navarre, which is under French jurisdiction.

Area and population

The Basque Country has an area of 20,000 square kilometres, less than that of Galicia or the Principality of Catalonia, each of which has an area of about 30,000 square kilometres. The area of Wales is 20,763 square kilometres.

The southern parts of the Basque Country, under Spanish jurisdiction, make up the greater part of this area, whereas the northern parts, under French authority, make up only a little more than a tenth (14%). The province of Álava alone is as extensive as the northern Basque Country. The province of Navarra (as the southern part is called in Castilian) makes up half of the Basque territory. The other six provinces can be divided, by area, into two groups: the three southern provinces, each consisting of between 10% and 15% of the total, and the three northern provinces, each of which takes up between 4% and 6%. In terms of surface area, Álava is the largest and Basse Navarre the smallest province.

Since the total area of the Spanish State is of the order of 500,000 square kilometres, the southern Basque Country represents 3.5% of the whole, and given that the area of the French State is approximately 550,000 square kilometres, the northern Basque Country occupies only 0.5%. Wales has an area that is a little more than 8% of the United Kingdom's.

According to the most recent Censuses, the population of the

Basque Country is 2,873,512, of whom 254,194 live in the northern part (Census of 15 March 1990) and 2,623,318 in the south (Census of 1 March 1991). The population of Wales at the 1991 Census was 2,835,073, about 5% of the population of the United Kingdom.

The population of the northern provinces represents less than a tenth of that of the Basque Country as a whole. So by density of population they are only half as important as they are in territorial terms. The most populous districts in the north are to be found along the coast between Bayonne (Baiona) and Hendaye (Hendaia), where almost the entire population lives.

As far as the south is concerned, the population is nearer that of Galicia, but is only about half that of the Principality of Catalonia. Among the four provinces of the southern Basque Country, Vizcaya's population alone makes up almost half. If Navarra is not taken into account, it is Vizcaya which has the greatest number of inhabitants.

The population of the northern Basque Country accounts for 0.4% of the population of the French State, while that of the southern provinces makes up 7.5% of the population of the Spanish State. The density of population is very high in the provinces of Vizcaya and Guipúzcoa, both of which are heavily industrialized, followed by Labourd where the tourist industry of the northern coast is concentrated.

As a consequence of the lack of political unity and a co-ordinated economic policy, the Basque Country has been developed in a very uneven way, which has caused obvious inequalities between the various zones, and this in turn is highlighted by variations in the density of population.

The Basque Country has five important centres, among which Bilbao (Bilbo) stands out with nearly half a million inhabitants, or more if we take into account the communities of what is called Greater Bilbao. Each of the other three centres of the southern Basque Country — Pamplona (Irunea), San Sebastián (Donostia) and Vitoria (Gazteiz) — has about 170,000 inhabitants. The fifth most important centre is Bayonne, in the north, with 50,000 inhabitants. Besides these large centres, we should bear in mind the role played throughout history by a number of smaller regional centres, namely those of the valleys and districts.

Three political strata

The seven provinces of the Basque Country are not united in a single political institution but are divided into three distinct parts: on one side the three northern provinces, on the other the three southern provinces, and Navarra south of the Pyrénées. The northern Basque Country, which is part of the French State, does not form a *département* of its own, but is included, with the Béarn, in the *département* of Pyrénées-Atlantiques, of which the *préfecture* is situated in Pau, the capital of the Béarn, Bayonne being only a *sous-préfecture*.

Among the policies put forward by the late François Mitterand in the 1981 Election campaign, which led to his becoming President of the French Republic, was the promise of a Basque *département*. Once victory had been won, and despite numerous reminders, the new French President consistently refused to honour his electoral pledge. Indeed, today as in former times, the Basque provinces under French rule are deprived of all legal status: they have neither a *département* nor an electoral constituency, neither a judicial district nor a university. In short, they have no administrative powers whatsoever.

Perhaps we should refer, as it offered a glimmer of hope for the future, to the formation in 1994 of an Elected Council for the northern Basque Country and of a Development Council which, although it has only consultative powers, is concerned with the Basque areas on the French side of the border.

The three western provinces of the Basque Country, that is to say Álava, Guipúzcoa and Vizcaya, have been known throughout their history as *'provincias vascongadas'*. This is due to the fact that in ancient times, according to one theory, they came under the influence of their western neighbours, the Basques of Navarra. Since the accord signed on 17 July 1979 between the Madrid Government and the *PNV* and, more officially, since the referendum on autonomy which was held in these three provinces on 25 October in that same year, the territory has been designated one of the seventeen Autonomous Regions of the Spanish State, and is known as the *Comunidad Autónoma Vasco* (The Autonomous Basque Community); we shall refer to it by its initials, *CAV*. Its capital is the town of Vitoria.

Furthermore, Navarra south of the Pyrénées has become another of these Autonomous Regions and is known as the *Comunidad Foral Navarra* (The Foral Community of Navarra). The law under which it came into existence is known as the *Amejoramiento del Fuero Navarro*. Signed in Madrid in March 1982 by representatives of Navarra and those of the Spanish Government, it was approved a few days later by the Parliament of Navarra and then by the Assembly of Deputies in Madrid on 30 June 1982. The word *fors*, which comes from the Latin word for 'forum', a place where justice was administered, has been traditionally used in the Basque Country to denote the native laws or charters.

Down the centuries, the main divide between Basque institutions has been that between the northern and southern parts of the country. As a result of the creation of the *CAV*, there is now a divide between the western provinces and Navarra. The law known as the *Amejoramiento* has only deepened this divide. As a consequence of all this, since 1982 the Basque Country has been politically carved into three parts which we shall call the North, the *CAV*, and Navarra.

The various institutions of the three parts

We shall now review the institutions of each of the three parts of the Basque Country, in order to clarify the electoral responsibilities which the population is called upon to exercise.

As we have already said, the northern Basque Country is incorporated with the Béarn in the *département* of Pyrénées-Atlantiques. It is an irony of fate that the General Council, the body responsible for the *département*'s administration, meets in the same building as the Parliament of Navarre, which was also in former times the seat of the *Cortes* of Navarre, in the town of Pau. This *département* elects, with four others in south-western France, the Regional Council of Aquitaine, a parliamentary body which is responsible for the administration of the region and meets at Bordeaux.

As for the *CAV*, it comprises three provincial mini-parliaments, the so-called *Juntas Generales* (each composed of 51 members), whose main function is to formulate and control the *Diputación* or Executive Committee of each province. There is also, for all three provinces, the Autonomous Parliament of Vitoria (with 75 members), a legislative body, on which the government of the Basque Country depends. This last is a misnomer, since it excludes the other Basque territories, Navarra and the northern provinces.

The Foral Community of Navarre, because it has provincial functions, has a single legislative body, the Parliament of Navarra, with 50 members, on which the government of Navarra relies. This province also has another institution of its own which embraces a much less important unit, the *Concejo*, which represents the inhabitants of a locality, whether it is a densely populated area, or one which, in its time, had a separate existence but is now merged with others, and is an important centre with its own history. Members of the *Concejos* are elected at the same time as local elections are held.

Electoral confusion

The Basques on either side of the Franco-Spanish border vote in elections for no fewer than a dozen different institutions: the Town Hall, the *Concejo* (in Navarra), the General Council of Pyrénées-Atlantiques, the *Juntas Generales* of the three western provinces, the Foral Parliament of Navarre, the Autonomous Parliament of Vitoria, the General Council of Aquitaine, the Spanish Congress and Senate, the French National Assembly, the Presidency of the French Republic, and the European Parliament. This is surely too many for such a small country, especially since instead of promoting unity, this plethora of institutions weakens and destroys it.

In each of these distinct parts of the country, the citizen votes for representation at six levels, although these levels and institutions will vary from one territory to the next. The only institution and election in which all three parts of the Basque Country come together are those for the European Parliament, though again the north and the south vote in different constituencies.

The six ballots in the northern Basque Country have no bearing on the French Senate, which is not directly elected by the voters but indirectly by elected representatives every nine years. The elections for the General Council of the *département* are called 'cantonals' because each councillor is elected to represent one of the electoral cantons or divisions. The cantons are therefore electoral districts which generally include more than one commune (if these are small); sometimes, however, if the canton is a large one, it is limited to this single commune, or even to a part of it. The cantonal elections take place every three years, but on each occasion only half the representatives stand for election, so that at each cantonal election only half the cantons cast their vote. The French municipal elections take place every six years, those for the French Assembly and the European Parliament every five years, while the Presidential Election takes place every seven years and the Regional Elections every six years.

In the southern Basque Country the six ballots take place in only four elections because in four of them, two votes are cast at the same time. At the legislative elections there is one ballot for the Town Hall and another for the *Juntas Generales* (in the western provinces) or for the Parliament of Navarra. There are no Presidential Elections, because Spain has a King rather than a President. Elections for the Spanish State (Congress and Senate), and for the municipalities, take place every four years, and for the European Parliament every five years, as in all other member-States of the European Union. In the three western provinces, the election of the *Juntas Generales*, held on the same day as the municipal elections, as well as those of the Autonomous Parliament, take place every four years. In Navarra, the election of members to the Parliament and to the *Concejos* is held on the same day as the municipal elections, every four years.

The official districts

We have seen that, in its division into political districts, the Basque Country does not enjoy any political unity. We also need to put on record now that neither in any other sphere, that is to say among those institutions which are not political in the strict sense, such as the Army, the Catholic Church, the University, and so on, is the Basque identity recognized. The only association which covers the Basque Country in its entirety is *Euskalzaindia*, the Academy of the Basque Language. All other bodies set limits to their work without taking into account the country's territorial integrity.

As far as the northern provinces are concerned, the various branches of the French Army, the judicial system, the university, ecclesiastical organization, and so on, are all based on areas which are larger than the Basque territory. Notable exceptions are the Chamber of Commerce at Bayonne, which for some years now has included the whole of the northern Basque Country, and also the Elected Council and the Development Council, both established in 1994.

As for the southern parts of the country, only a few educational bodies and sporting federations, such as the *Real Automóvil Club*, and scarcely any other, take the Basque territory into account in their use of the term *basco-navarrais*. The Jesuits also recognize it, since the province of Loyola coincides with the boundaries of the southern Basque Country. More institutions recognized this entity under the Franco regime than since the advent of democracy.

The Spanish Army includes the southern Basque Country with other Spanish provinces, in the fifth military region, that of the Western Pyrénées, of which the capital is Burgos. For the Navy it is included in the vast *'zona del Cantabrico'* with its centre at El Ferrol. For the Air Force it is part of its third zone which takes in all the north-east of the peninsula, with its headquarters at Zaragoza. Military tribunals lump the southern Basque Country with the entire north-west of the peninsula.

As for the Catholic Church, it divides the southern part of the country into two separate archbishoprics. One includes Guipúzcoa, Navarra, La Rioja and part of Aragón, while the other takes in

Vizcaya, Álava, Burgos, Palencia and Soria. When in November 1982 Pope Jean-Paul II visited the Basque Country, the media were on the alert to see whether, on touching down, he would kneel and kiss the soil of Loyola, as he was wont to do in other places. Such a gesture would have amounted to a recognition of Basque territoriality. But he did not make it.

Judicial responsibilities correspond today with political autonomy, so that the Basque Country possesses a *Tribunal Superior de Justicia del País Vasco* with its headquarters at Bilbao, as does Navarra, both of which have territorial control of questions relating to civil and penal law. The picture is even more complicated when it comes to administrative districts. For example, any problem involving water supplies in the province of Guipúzcoa, which belongs to the Hydrographic Confederation of Northern Spain, has to be dealt with by the *Tribunal Superior de Justicia* at Oviedo, the Confederation's judicial capital. On the other hand, if the problem concerns Navarra, which belongs to the Hydrographic Confederation of the Ebro, the appropriate court will be located there. Much the same is true for all other administrative matters. The universities come under the umbrella of the various autonomous structures of the Spanish State, so that there is one for the *CAV* and another for Navarra.

In matters involving the police, there has been some measure of adaptation, at least in that part of the peninsula which is called *'Estado de las Autonomas'*: one police district corresponds to the *CAV* and another to Navarra. The only official recognition of the totality of the southern Basque Country is a police project, known since 1983 as the *Plan Zen (Zona Especial Norte)*, which we shall look at in more detail in Chapter 7; it unites all four provinces in the fight against *ETA*.

This caricature, this official non-recognition, is also to be seen in the realm of sport, for the Basque Country is unable to play football at international level, as do Wales and Scotland, for example. The same applies to all other sports, including those which are authentically Basque such as *pelota*.

Chapter 2

THE SLOW DEATH OF AN ANCIENT LANGUAGE

'The Basque language,' wrote the linguist Koldo Mitxelena, 'is a small language, that is to say comparatively not very extensive, which survives in a community which is itself restricted to the western part of the Pyrénées and the Gulf of Biscay, on both sides of the Franco-Spanish border.'

The Basque word for the language is *euskara*. It is sometimes said that Basque, which is indigenous to the area where it is spoken today and which has no known connections with any other language, is the oldest language in Europe. What is meant when we say that Basque is the oldest language in Europe, since all languages are derived one from another and, ultimately and in a certain sense, each is as ancient as the others? It means that Basque is the only pre-Indo-European language spoken in Europe today. The language was already in existence during the Bronze Age, some two thousand years before the birth of Christ, when Indo-European tribes who were familiar with agriculture and the use of the wheel began to move into Europe. Almost all European languages are derived from this Indo-European source, whether they belong to the Latin, Germanic, Slavonic or Celtic groups, or to the smaller groups such as Greek or Albanian. Some other languages, like Magyar, Estonian, Lapp and Finnish, do not belong to this common stock at all, but they arrived in Europe after the Indo-European invasion. The only language which arrived prior to the invasion was Basque. This means that the Basque language is the oldest in Europe. The others may also be considered as having great antiquity, but not within the borders of Europe. The Basque language is the sole survivor of those languages which were spoken on the continent before the arrival of the Indo-Europeans about 4,000 years ago.

The Basque language is autochthonous to the territory in which it is spoken today. 'On this territory,' wrote Mitxelena, 'an ancient form of Basque was in use during the early centuries of our era.' There is no evidence of any other language which was spoken on this territory before the Basque language. Basque is a rare case of a language which has no known linguistic relations, and that is why it is considered to be unique. There have been various attempts to establish possible links with many other languages, in particular with Iberian and certain Caucasian and North African languages, but nothing has yet been proven. It is not that the language was unrelated to any other, for at some time in the past it must have been, like all languages; nor simply that all the languages to which Basque was related are dead; but rather that they disappeared as recognizable linguistic systems so long ago that it is exceedingly difficult to find traces of them in modern European languages.

The Basque-speaking area

Not all the Basque Country is Basque-speaking. The provinces of Guipúzcoa, Labourd, Basse Navarre and Soule (see diagram 6) belong almost wholly to what we may call the Basque-speaking area. On the other hand, there are parts of the provinces of Álava, Navarra and Vizcaya where Basque is not spoken.

Diagrams 5 and 6 show the changes in the Basque-speaking area during the last two thousand years. It will be observed that this area has been slowly and more or less continuously retreating for centuries. Over the last two hundred years the language's decline has been much more rapid in the southern part of the Basque Country, under Spanish control, than in the northern part, which is under French jurisdiction. Up to the change in dynasty, from the Hapsburgs to the Bourbons, which took place in Spain in 1701, this retreat would probably have been brought about by natural causes, that is to say as a consequence of the spontaneous struggle between languages, rather than as a result of a deliberate policy dictated by Madrid which had as its aim the sapping of the Basque language's vitality.

Nevertheless, it is symptomatic that the Spaniard Antonio de Nebrija noted in the prologue to the first grammar of the Castilian language, published during the reign of the Catholic Kings, in 1492 (the same year as the conquest of Granada and the discovery of America): 'Not only the enemies of our faith must acquaint themselves with the Castilian language, but also the people of Vizcaya and Navarra, the French and the Italians, and all those who have business in Spain and therefore need to know our language, and if they do not speak it as their native tongue, they will now be able the more easily to learn it, by means of my book.' From this we may conclude that the first Spanish grammar had among its objectives the teaching of the language to the people of Navarra and Vizcaya who, at that time, must have had a very imperfect knowledge of it, since they spoke mainly Basque. However, the accession to the throne of the Bourbon King Philip V marked the inauguration of a linguistic policy that was intended to encourage the expansion throughout the State's territory of a single language, Castilian, at the expense of all others.

In 1717, Philip V responded to a series of petitions, some to do with language, which had been presented to him by the people of Majorca, by urging them 'to introduce the Castilian language into the island's villages'. In the same year he addressed to the *corregidores* of Catalonia a secret decree which included the sentence: 'The *corregidor* will take the greatest care to introduce the Castilian language, using the most moderate and discreet methods, so that only the result will be noticeable and not the means' (Josep Melia, *Informe sobre la lengua catalana*, 1970).

The handling of the language question was not, however, consistent during the course of the 18th, 19th and 20th centuries. Although the policies of Madrid and Paris were always, more or less discreetly, hostile towards the Basque language, the outward signs of these policies sometimes revealed a more deliberate intention. For example, we may quote the opinion of the historian Roger Collins, who can hardly be suspected of having sympathy with the Basques, when in his book *Los Vascos* (Alianza Editorial, 1989) he wrote that 'on both sides of the border there was pressure to make the Basques more fully French or Spanish. Already in the 19th century the use of Basque on the Spanish side was being discouraged, so that this process was not something introduced in the years immediately following the Civil War.' Roger Collins also refers to 'the increasing influx of population more recently encouraged by a central Government which sees in the unique racial and linguistic heritage of the Basques a threat to the national unity of Spain'.

Let us also recall a well-known practice, at least during the first decades of the century that is now drawing to a close. At the beginning of each school day, a ring was given to a pupil who was required to pass it on to any other child caught speaking Basque. The pupil with the ring in his possession at the end of the afternoon was beaten. By such means, the use of Basque was actively discouraged in the schools. It should be added that, at various times and in certain places, this practice won the approval of parents, who had been conditioned by the attitudes of officialdom and its local representatives.

We shall not try to describe here the vicissitudes and subtleties of linguistic policy carried out during the last hundred years or so, for it is too large a subject. We should, nevertheless, note that if it was generally of a discreet nature at the outset, it later took on a more explicit form, as a consequence of the establishment of the Franco regime to the south of the Pyrénées. The Spanish State prohibited all public signs in Basque, as well as the civil registration of children with Basque names, such as 'Iñaki, Kepa, Koldobika and all others which flagrantly smack of separatism', as a decree of 1938 put it. The Academy of the Basque Language, founded in 1918, was officially recognized only in 1976, after the dictator's death.

The fact is that, for all these reasons, the Basque-speaking area is today restricted to the territory shown in Diagram 6. A small part of Basse Navarre, a somewhat larger part of Vizcaya, a very important part of Navarra and particularly of Álava, are therefore excluded. It must also be noted that four of the five main Basque centres, namely Bayonne, Bilbao, Pamplona and Vitoria, are also excluded. San Sebastián is the only centre of any importance which belongs to the Basque-speaking area.

The number of Basque-speakers

The most serious implication for the fate of the Basque language is perhaps not the retreat of the Basque-speaking area but the language's rapid decline within that area. Indeed, whereas the usual maps showing details of the language, including our own diagrams, take account of its territorial retreat in chronological terms they do not convey much idea of its decreasing incidence within the Basque-speaking area itself. Although in reality the two processes go hand-in-hand, the second is much more serious than the first.

In order to understand the level of the language's concentration in the Basque provinces, we must first of all acquaint ourselves with the number of Basque-speakers, and then compare that with the population as a whole.

The estimate carried out more than a century ago by Ladislao de Velasco reminds us that in his day more than half the inhabitants of the seven provinces spoke Basque. Nearly all the people of Vizcaya and Guipúzcoa were Basque-speaking, as were about half the inhabitants of the Basque Country on the French side of the frontier, a fifth of the people of Navarra and 12% of those of Álava.

This proportion (54% in 1868) had been reduced to 23.7% by 1991, as can be seen in the following table taken from the yearbook *Euskadi 1993* published by the newspaper *Egin*. For the southern parts of the Basque Country, the information regarding the number of Basque-speakers is taken from the Census of 1991, while for the northern parts they come from a survey carried out by the firm known as Siadeco in 1990.

Numbers and percentages of Basque-speakers (1991):

Area	Population	Basque-speakers	Percentage
Álava	272,447	25,300	9.3
Basse Navarre	29,298	18,897	64.5
Guipúzcoa	676,488	310,100	45.8
Labourd	204,598	53,195	26.0
Navarra	519,277	52,023	10.0
Vizcaya	1,155,106	212,600	18.4
Soule	16,298	8,915	54.7
Total	2,873,512	681,030	23.7

To recapitulate, at the present time 23.7% of the population of the Basque Country are able to speak Basque, and more in certain provinces than in others. (The percentage of speakers among the inhabitants of the 'Basque-speaking area', not counting those in the areas where the language is not generally spoken, is of course somewhat higher.)

During the course of the 19th century the decline in the percentage of Basque-speakers was larger in the south of the country than in the north, due to different rates of industrialization, the south having attracted a great mass of Spanish-speaking workers. The fall in this percentage of Basque-speakers among the population as a whole did not remain constant throughout this period, however, for in recent years there has been an encouraging upward trend in the south of the country. The Censuses carried out since 1981 have included a question regarding knowledge of the Basque language. That of 1981 asked this question in Álava, Guipúzcoa and Vizcaya, those of 1986 and 1991 asked it in Navarra. Unfortunately, the Census in the northern parts of the Basque Country, under the jurisdiction of the French State, has never collected linguistic information, so that we are denied statistical knowledge of what has been happening there.

As far as the southern parts of the country are concerned, the proportion of Basque-speakers has been of the order of 21.5% in 1981, 24.5% in 1986 and 26% in 1991; this information relates only to the three provinces of Álava, Guipuzkoa and Vizcaya. Of the four provinces of the southern Basque Country (that is to say the three already mentioned plus Navarra) we can say that the proportion of Basque-speakers has been as follows: 21.7% in 1986 and 22.9% in 1991. It is clear then that, according to recent Censuses, the percentage of Basque-speakers has increased throughout the southern parts of the country in recent decades, which is no doubt an encouraging sign for those who work on the language's behalf.

However, the statistics provided by the Census may be unreliable: Basques have a tendency to over-estimate their knowledge of the language. Unfortunately, the authorities prefer not to take into account the degree of distortion which is produced by Censuses in this respect, although the phenomenon is well-known in general if not in its detailed effects. It is difficult to see, for example, how the number of Basque-speakers in Álava has increased from 9,700 to 25,300 between 1981 and 1991, or how nearly two-thirds of Basque-speakers are able to write the language, as the official statistics seem to suggest. Nevertheless, we believe that the Census statistics allow a degree of optimism with regard to the recent growth in the number of Basque-speakers.

The use of the Basque language

That speakers of Basque use it for only part of their daily lives results in a more restricted use of the language than an objective analysis of the Basque-speaking area or the number of Basque-speakers might at first suggest. In effect, the process of using more than one language usually has three phases: in the first, people know only the original language; in the second, they know both languages; and in the third they know only the language which takes the place of the original language. Until quite recently a part of the population was monolingual in Basque, but this group has recently disappeared and there are now only those who are monolingual in Spanish or French (the great majority of the population) and the bilinguals who speak Basque as well as Spanish or French, and who, as we have seen, make up 23.7% of the population.

As a consequence, it has become virtually impossible to live with competence only in Basque, whereas it is possible — and even commonly the case — to live with a knowledge of only Spanish or French. The Basque-speaker is obliged to use the other language in at least part of his daily life, not only for legal reasons but also because of his language's inferior social status.

It emerges from the 5,300 interviews carried out in 1991 through-out the Basque Country at the request of the *CAV* and published in the magazine *Jakin* at the end of 1993, that about half of Basque-speakers converse more comfortably in Basque than in Spanish or French, and that the other half are more at home in one of the other languages. This is clearly a consequence of the ascendancy of Spanish and French and of the linguistic policies implemented by their re-spective Governments.

Linguistic facility apart, there is another much stronger factor which reduces the practical use of the Basque language to a level lower than what one might expect from the number of individuals who can speak it. In any group conversing in Basque it is very probable that one or other among the speakers will not know the language, especially if the group has any status, and in this case the conversation generally slips into Spanish, or into French as the case may be. These two factors explain the fact that according to the survey previously mentioned, only about half (53%) of Basque-speaking families usually speak the language at home and that this proportion drops to 44% when the Basque-speaker visits his friends and to 37% when he is at work.

In 1989 a language association had the excellent idea of assessing the use of Basque in the streets of the country's main towns, those with more than 10,000 inhabitants, where some 70% of the popula-tion is concentrated. The results of the survey were as follows: only a small proprtion (42%) spoke Basque in the street, the rest (58%) choosing to speak Spanish or French; the source for these figures is the yearbook *Euskadi 1991*.

All this refers to the use of the language by those who can speak it and not to the population as a whole. If the entire population is taken into account, then among those who participated in the survey only 7.6% were Basque-speaking. What is true of the survey, which was carried out on behalf of the *CAV* in the larger towns, also holds good for the country as a whole, both north and south.

Unfortunately, the latter survey — based on interviews in the street — is an isolated one, and we have no comparable studies on which to base an opinion as to whether the use of Basque (and not merely a theoretical knowledge of it) is on the increase or decrease. Our personal experience leads us to believe that probably there has been a slow but relentless decline over the years. A simple stroll through the squares and streets of various villages and towns in the Basque Country will give some indication, albeit impressionistic, of the fact that Basque, as the language of everyday life, is now more or less in its death-throes. It seems as if the Basque language is tending at the present time to transform itself into a language of academic culture and gradually abandoning its role as an everyday, living language. Only a great co-ordinated effort on the part of those who wish to safeguard it can ensure that it avoids this fate.

The President of the Basque Nationalist Party (*PNV*), Xavier Arzalluz, writing in the newspaper *Deia* on 13 December 1987, commented that the Basque language 'is living in a state not precisely of retreat but one of mortal agony'.

We may sum up the foregoing paragraphs by saying that the Basque Country is not entirely Basque-speaking, that not all its inhabitants speak the language, and lastly that not all those who are Basque-speaking use the language most of the time. Some would claim that the Basque language is slowly making progress, that it is gradually emerging from its state of secular marginalization. All the evidence, however, leads us to the conclusion that those who think thus are being over-optimistic and spend more time in their offices than in the real world. The deplorable situation of the Basque language, of which the Basques themselves are aware — in a somewhat diffuse but widespread way — is doubtless one of the most important causes of their grievances and recrimination against the political authorities which tolerate such a situation, and this is a very strong reason for their revolt. The language provides the Basques with their main feeling of collective identity. Furthermore, this sense of identity, despite the fact that it has not found a place in the dominant political scheme of things, whether on the Right or Left, takes on — as among all peoples who speak a minority language — an over-riding importance.

In order to understand this feeling, it can be compared with that of an individual who has a place in a political scheme of things which recognizes individuals but not peoples. If someone were to be asked whether he would like to enjoy the same health as another person, to be as beautiful, as youthful, or as well-off, he would doubtless reply in the affirmative. But if he were to be asked whether he would like to become that other person, he would reply that he would certainly not. Each individual wishes to have the advantages enjoyed by others, but without becoming them, without renouncing his own self. This feeling of identity is well understood at the individual level but not at the collective, or so it would seem; it is, however, a simple, elementary and potent feeling.

The language is not the only badge of Basque identity. Among other markers are sports, dance, customs, cuisine, festivals, and psycho-cultural characteristics such as a particular sense of humour and the rituals associated with death and bereavement. But it is the language which is the essence of Basque identity. All countries can boast a famous writer who has expressed in one way or another the idea that 'my language is my country' with reference to his own tongue. As far as Basque is concerned, this idea is doubly true: it is rooted in the public mind and in ancient tradition.

The growth in the teaching of Basque

The foreign observer who takes an interest in the Basque Country usually subscribes to the general view that, since the death of Franco, the children and young people of this country receive an education through the medium of the Basque language or that, at the very least, by the time they have finished their compulsory schooling, they will have succeeded in learning the language. Nothing could be further from the truth.

Let us take as a basis for observation the period of compulsory education for children from six to fourteen, which in our opinion is the one in which the acquisition of the language takes place. In the northern parts of the country, in the three provinces under the jurisdiction of the French State, only 1.4% of children receive an education in the Basque language, and this is in the schools known as *ikastolak*, which are private Basque-medium schools encouraged and promoted by parents for patriotic reasons. The public schools and the private schools run by the Church, on the other hand, have long since dispensed education exclusively in French, although more recently, bilingual classes have been created to meet the demands of parents' associations such as *Ikas-Bi*.

In the southern parts, those under the Spanish State, pupils between six and fourteen are to be found in three groups, according to the language in which they are being educated. The first receive their education mainly in Castilian (58.3%); the second group are taught half in Castilian and half in Basque (19.5%); and the third mainly in Basque (22.2%). These figures relate to all schools, whether public, religious or private, and include the *ikastolak*, in the academic year 1991-92.

This means that 58.3% of children in the southern Basque Country who complete their compulsory education by the age of fourteen cannot speak Basque and that only 41.7% can. It is important to underline that this second group is in a minority position, albeit a sizeable one, and that the majority of pupils finish their schooling without gaining a knowledge of Basque.

The gravity of these figures, which are unusual for a European country, is partly off-set by the fact that the proportion of pupils learning Basque during their school years has continued to grow in recent years: we have seen a slow but encouraging process by which a system that has not taken the language into account is being replaced by others in which it is taught.

Given that we have data only for the three provinces which make up the *CAV*, we must note here that if in1991-92 the proportion of pupils learning Basque was of the order of 48.4%, it used to be, in 1982-83, 18.9%. During the last ten years or so, the growth-rate has therefore been slow but constant, the result of a determined and productive effort on the part of those campaigning for education through the medium of Basque. (Strictly speaking, in the absence of data for Navarra, the proportion of Basque learners should be 41.7% rather than 48.7%.)

However, positive trends in the evolution of the Basque language are not limited to the contexts to which we have been able to point so far, namely the growing proportion of Basque-speakers within the population as a whole, according to the Census returns, and the increasing proportion of pupils who attend schools where the language is taught. There are other signs of recovery, although they may not be so quantifiable, such as the existence of a television channel broadcasting exclusively in Basque. Established after the creation of the *CAV*, its programmes can be seen over a large part of the northern provinces and Navarra, as well as by viewers in the three provinces of the Autonomous Community. The territory is also served by half-a-dozen radio stations broadcasting exclusively in Basque. The publishing of books in the language, too, has seen a remarkable development, as much in the number of titles published as in the choice of reading material now available. Since 1990 there has been a daily newspaper printed in Basque which takes its place with a number of magazines already in existence.

Other facts would no doubt contribute to our description of the Basque language at the present time, but we think that those already given are enough to convey an overall view.

Official support for the Basque language

Since the French Revolution of 1789, the authorities in the northern parts of the Basque Country have pursued a policy of active opposition to all languages other than French, by means of the school, the civil service, the system of communications, and by all other legal measures.

As the speaking of Basque began gradually to decline in these northern provinces, there were some instances of cautious official support for the language, such as the rather feeble help given to those schools where it was taught, whether to children or adults. But these instances were clearly insignificant in both their number and in financial terms. Even if it were not for the insufficiency of these concessions, it would have been helpful if a general plan of official aid for the language had been implemented as a first step towards linguistic recovery. That, however, would have required local authorities which, despite all appearances to the contrary, were willing to take an interest in the matter. We shall come back to the question of a plan for the language in the next chapter.

We could speak of a similar situation in the southern parts of the country, in Navarra, where the authorities have offered support to an ailing language only for as long as it struggles to take its last gasp, but have hardly helped to put it on the road to recovery. The Basque Language Law approved by the Parliament of Navarra in 1986 divides the province into three zones, according to the strength of the Basque language. It establishes certain rights relating to the learning and use of the language in public which are in direct proportion to the number of Basque-speakers in each zone. But these provisions have turned out to be quite inadequate.

The third part of the country, the *CAV,* pursues a rather more favourable and active policy in defence of the language. This is not due to the fact that Basque is more widely spoken there — Basse Navarre has the highest proportion of speakers and Álava has the lowest — but because greater public pressure on behalf of the language exists there, which is to be seen in the more substantial vote for Nationalist candidates at the elections.

We may cite as a significant example of neglect on the part of the *CAV* its refusal up to 1994 to offer official recognition and support for the impressive organization known as *AEK*, which works for the co-ordination of teaching Basque to adults and has centres in all seven provinces.

The reason for the Government's attitude, which was generally deplored by the public, was that — although this may seem implausible — the directorate of *AEK* was not under its control and maintained a political stance that was much more radical. Fortunately, without offering any explanation for its change in attitude, in 1994 the *CAV* reached an agreement with the directorate of *AEK* and now co-operates with it.

Another similar example of the same sad initial attitude and eventually a happier outcome is that of the daily newspaper *Egunka-*

ria, to which for many years no support was given at all. Published by one of the municipal authorities within the *CAV*, and distributed generally, it takes an openly pluralistic line and is the only one to be published exclusively in Basque. What is more, whereas the authorities paid for official advertisements to be printed in dailies published in Spanish, they refused to do the same for the Basque paper, which resulted in a serious loss of revenue and income for its staff. In the interests of the Basque language, the *CAV* put an end to this contentious and inexplicable policy in 1994, and so, as far as official support is concerned, the newspaper has set out on a course of normalization which will lead to its achieving equality with the other dailies published within the Autonomous Community.

The Basque-medium Summer University (*UEU*) also finds itself in financial straits at the present time. This initiative at tertiary level began in the 1970s as part of the Bayonne Cultural Festival. Held at the outset in the northern part of the country, it has now moved to Pamplona. To this important organization, which receives only meagre subsidy, we owe the publication of more than 180 books in the Basque language for use at university level. In all three cases — *AEK, Egunkaria,* and the *UEU* — the lack of sensitivity on the part of the authorities has been compensated, as on so many occasions in the history of the Basque Country, by the effort and selfless sacrifice of the public, ready at all times to defend the language as the supreme badge of its identity.

The general attitude of the *CAV* in linguistic matters has been about as tactless as it is possible to be. Instead of supporting the public bodies which already exist — they have a vigour of which other minority languages in Europe have cause to be envious — the authorities have tried to create official bodies to replace them. Not having succeeded, they have at last given in, but too late and grudgingly.

The people of the Basque Country have always been ahead of the authorities in their zeal for the support of the language of their forefathers. It was as a result of the experiments taking place in Guipúzcoa a decade earlier, during the 1960s and in the heyday of the Franco regime, that the movement known as the *ikastolak*, or private Basque-medium schools, at first run clandestinely but later tolerated, although never actively supported by the authorities, came into existence. Many thousands of Basque families, by their devotion and financial support, have been involved in this experiment, which is unique in Europe and has now spread to all parts of the country. In 1991-92 the schools in the southern parts were providing education for no fewer than 17% of pupils. They have given an opportunity for a whole generation, or at least part of it, to acquire and master a language that had been consigned to the scrap-heap. If these schools had not been created, it would have meant a catastrophe for the transmission of the language among those who grew up under Franco. Although the *ikastolak* movement has recently been hamstrung by the authorities in a most shameful manner, largely through the imposition of crippling financial conditions, the importance of this popular scheme and its serious contribution to the transmission of the language during a very difficult phase of its history, remains incontrovertible.

The basis for a new linguistic policy

In such achievements as the creation of Basque television and radio, and so on, we may recognize institutions which are doubtless necessary and of a positive nature. But if the Basque language is to recover from the ailments from which it is suffering, the linguistic policies now being adopted by the authorities will have to be considerably modified and implemented in diffferent ways. Otherwise, Basque will continue to decline as a spoken language that is used in everyday life, gradually and imperceptibly. This process can be compared with the hands of a watch, the movement of which cannot be seen by the human eye but which is nevertheless unceasing, for time never stops.

If, however, this process appears to be imperceptible, it is not really : it only seems to be so because we do not have the means by which it might be measured. In order to trace the evolution of the Basque language, some money will certainly have to be spent, although only a small sum would be needed. Using modern methods, it should be possible to take accurate measurements of the language's positive or negative evolution over recent decades, just as price-levels and other complex phenomena can be measured. But the authorities prefer to adopt a triumphalist attitude, giving the impression that the Basque language is making progress, 'slowly but surely', rather than applying the appropriate gauges and frankly recognizing that, by following this course of action, the patient is slowly dying. They choose not to know — 'everything's looking fine' — instead of carrying out today the scientific evaluations needed if recovery is to be ensured tomorrow.

What are the measures that must be adopted if a linguistic policy aimed at normalizing the situation of the Basque language is to be put in hand? The first would be to refuse to go on allowing the legal inequality from which Basque suffers in comparison with Spanish and French. In their respective States, including the Basque Country north and south, these two languages are obligatory and official, while Basque on its own territory is merely optional. The acquisition of Basque is simply a question of the individual's goodwill, whereas the learning of the other two is a legal necessity.

How can we talk of full bilingualism while this principle of inequality continues to exist? Inequality of the sexes or the races — or inequality in any other context, for that matter — is certainly difficult to overcome for a thousand reasons, but it is quite impossible to achieve real equality if the point of departure is inequality before the law. The consequences of all this for the fortunes of the Basque language are as numerous as they are negative: education in Castilian for all pupils and bilingual education for only some, and an administrative system carried on exclusively in Spanish, and so on. Equality in law will not be enough in itself to save the language, but it is nevertheless a necessity if we are to make the attempt.

There are three ways of making sure that the Basque language does not suffer discrimination on its home territory: it alone must be compulsory, or it must be compulsory in the same way as Spanish or French are, or else none of them must be compulsory. Each of these three alternatives has its supporters and its detractors, but be that as it may, in one way or another the present discrimination must be removed.

The second measure which would make a serious contribution to the language's revival is a degree of co-operation between Government and non-Government bodies with an interest in Basque; there are now many of the latter and some have considerable influence, as we have seen. The associations involved in support for Basque have always been numerous and they rely on the enthusiasm of thousands of people who are devoted to the cause of the language. We should also note here the enormous public demonstrations which, from year to year, have brought spirit and momentum to the movements which work on behalf of the language, as well as financial support.

Despite all this, as the sociolinguist Iñaki Larrañaga wrote in the magazine *Herria 2000 Eliza* on the subject of these Basque-language associations, 'They have never been really accepted by officialdom. It is a regrettable fact that the political authorities have shown no intention of co-ordinating the work of these numerous groups. Co-ordination is necessary, not in order to absorb them, nor to get rid of them or take advantage of them in any way, but rather so that each might follow its own path without doing any harm to the others.'

It is possible that the Basque language might disappear, but it might also prove capable of grasping the last chance of revival and normalization. None of us knows which of these two possibilities is going to happen. What we do know for certain is that, if the latter is to be the case, it will be necessary to organize a general mobilization of opinion which will unite, with the same dynamic drive, the initiative of both public bodies and the popular will. The Basque language is in a difficult position at present, and without the help of such an initiative, it will find it much too difficult to make a comeback in the public sector.

The third measure is linguistic planning in which the authorities of all parts of the Basque Country would have to participate. All available resources need to be mustered in a sensible way, clear objectives and definite time-limits must be identified, and the means of achieving them defined. What we need is a plan similar to that used for energy development, the economic sector, the hospitals, and so on.

'The process by which the Basque language is being replaced by Spanish or French is now well advanced,' wrote Iñaki Larrañaga in the article from which we have already quoted. 'It has almost reached a point of no return. If this situation is to be reversed, given that the language is not yet dead, it is clear that some urgent measures need to be taken. It is not worth going on as at present and leaving things as they are. We must take special, stringent measures, if we really want to change things.' Furthermore, the new linguistic policies should not be postponed into the distant future, for in view of the grave situation in which the language finds itself at present, it could be that the remedy will arrive too late.

But there is also another reason. At the present time we can rely on public opinion to serve as a lever for putting in motion a great effort on the language's behalf. Let us not forget that, in every poll, questions about the language receive a positive response from about 80% of the population. This popular support cannot be guaranteed for ever. It could happen that the Basques will grow sick and tired of the present efforts being made on the language's behalf but which yield such poor results. If that were to happen, the maintenance of Basque as a living language would definitely be a lost cause. Only an effective linguistic policy which produces tangible results can keep the public's support alive and relevant.

A policy of 'diffusion' or a 'territorial' policy?

Everything that has been said so far takes its place within the context of a linguistic policy based on the principle of 'diffusion', that is to

say one which attempts to underpin and spread the minority language without assigning to it a territory in which it would be necessary for all practical purposes. This policy of 'diffusion' does not aim
at ensuring that the minority language is stronger than the majority
language, even on a small part of its territory. 'Languages can survive
and flourish,' wrote the linguist J.A.Laponce, 'only if they have their
own territories which are theirs alone, where communication takes
place in one language that unites all individuals in a single community and satisfies the various needs of all who participate in it.' If this
theory, which is shared by a number of other distinguished
sociolinguists, holds true, it condemns Basque to death, for the
language has no exclusive territory of its own. To safeguard against
this possibility, it will be necessary to establish not only a policy
based on the principle of 'diffusion', but also one of 'territoriality',
which would ensure for Basque its own territory, even if it were to
be on a reduced scale, but on which it would be a language for use
in absolutely all contexts. If such a policy were to be applied to the
entire country, it would amount to what already exists in Switzerland
or Belgium. If applied only to a small part, it could be compared with
the tiny areas of western Ireland known as the *Gaeltacht* (to which
we shall come back in Chapter 9) where it is just about possible to
live in Irish without any need for English.

A 'territorial' policy would protect the collective rights of Basque-
speakers, whereas the principle of 'diffusion' is concerned only with
the rights of the individual, and then only imperfectly, since any
citizen from some other part of the French or Spanish State has the
legal right to be addressed in his own language, even within what we
have called 'the Basque-speaking area', thus compelling public servants to be able to speak that language, usually to the detriment of
the minority language.

Independently from the theoretical discussion of whether or not
the 'territorial' principle is indispensable for the survival of Basque,
a group of municipal councils in the south of the country have begun
to come together with a view to establishing in their areas this kind
of support for their language, so that the aspirations of many
Basque-speakers to live their lives entirely through the language are
beginning to be realized. These councils make up the movement
known as *UEMA*, the initials in Basque of the Movement of Basque-
speaking Districts. Twenty councils are members at the moment:
nine in Guipúzcoa, eight in Vizcaya and three in Navarra; Álava and
the northern provinces have no representatives.

The Movement, founded in 1989, is made up of those districts
where the Basque-speaking population is 80% or more. There are

about a hundred of these districts, out of a total in the southern parts of the country of about five hundred, and their Basque-speaking population is approximately 100,000 out of a total of 600,000. They are all districts where the population is sparse. Their aims are as follows: the official designation of mayors and councillors who are able to speak Basque, the creation of linguistic resources to be shared among the various Town Halls which belong to the group; a refusal to deal with correspondence and documentation which have no Basque versions; the provision of signs in Basque; the appointment of Basque-speakers to posts as doctors, policemen, bank employees, and shop-assistants; and the organization of Basque language-courses for adults who wish to learn the language.The experiment now being carried out by these Basque-speaking districts is contributing to the normalization of the language in a small part of the country, lending it support in geographical terms and helping it to be spoken with competence in all walks of life, including in an administrative context. It is thus also contributing to the natural evolution of the language in these districts where it is free from the tremendous pressure exerted by Castilian. The Movement is supported by the three Nationalist parties: *Eusko Alkartasuna, Herri Batasuna*, and the *PNV*.

Chapter 3

THE GROWTH OF BASQUE
NATIONALISM

Since the beginning of its recorded history, there has always been in the Basque Country a vigorous defence of its national identity against attempts by Madrid and Paris to impose uniformity on it. At times this resistance has taken peaceful, political and cultural forms, and at others the Basques have resorted to armed struggle.

The following may be considered as instances of armed resistance: the defence of the Kingdom of Navarra at the turn of the 15th century, the Carlist Wars of the 19th, the Basque battalions in the Civil War of 1936-39, and the present violent campaign of *Euskadi Ta Askatasuna*, more generally known by its initials *ETA*. All these are essentially different from one another, but they have in common a concern for the defence of the customs and sovereignty of the Basque Country.

The defence of Basque political sovereignty really begins in modern times with Sabino Arana Goiri, a native of Vizcaya, who was the first to formulate and express Nationalist aspirations, who devised the Basque flag, and who founded in 1895 the *Partido Nacionalista Vasco* (The Basque Nationalist Party). The Basque flag, which he invented, consists of a red ground symbolizing the people, the green diagonals of the cross of St. Andrew, representing the traditional Basque laws, and a white cross, the symbol of Christianity. From about 1900 Sabino Arana began referring to the Basque Country as *Euzkadi*, a neologism composed of the root *euzko*, meaning Basque, and the suffix *di*, which implies the whole or the collectivity. He applied the name *Euzkadi* (nowadays we write it as *Euskadi*) to the totality of the seven Basque provinces.

The birth of the Basque Nationalist Party

Sabino Arana was born in 1865 into a Carlist family whose wealth was in shipyards. He himself was a Carlist (a supporter of Don Carlos and his descendants as the rightful Kings of Spain) up to 1882, when his brother Luis explained to him that the Basques had a country of their own. He devoted the next five years to studying Law in Barcelona, as well as the Basque language which was not his mother-tongue. On his return to Bilbao he began to carry out research into Basque history and, in 1892, published his first book, *Bizkaia por su independencia,* the nationalism of which was confined to the province of Vizcaya. Two years later he was arguing for the federation of all seven Basque territories. His most important work of theory is *El Partido Carlista y los Fueros Vascos Navarros,* which was published in 1897. In his famous statement of 1903, made from his home at Larrazabal, he proposed replacing the Carlist motto *'Dios y Fueros'* ('God and Rights') with the new, though very similar *'Dios y la Ley Vieja'* ('God and the Ancient Law'). His vision of the Basque Country was a very idealistic one and it had strong racist and religious overtones.

Between 1893 and 1895 Sabino Arana edited and published the magazine *Bizkaitarra*, which landed him in court on several occasions. In 1894 he founded an association of Nationalists which was banned in the year following by the Civil Governor, who considered it to be ' a danger to the Spanish nation'. The foundation of the *PNV* took place in 1895. In 1898 he stood as a candidate in the Provincial Elections, narrowly failing to win a seat. In the following year five Nationalist councillors were elected to the town council of Bilbao, along with representatives of other parties. He was imprisoned in 1902 for sending a telegram to the American President, congratulating him on granting independence to Cuba. The Nationalist councillors were sacked for having sent another telegram to the Argentinian Government in which they failed to make clear their allegiance to the Spanish State.

The 'father of Basque Nationalism' died in 1903 at the age of 38. The first decade of the 20th century saw the rapid growth of the Basque Nationalist Party in the four southern provinces. But from the outset the Party suffered from serious internecine tensions between militants who wanted independence and those of a more Spanish regionalist tendency who found their recruits among the influential industrialists of Vizcaya. The Party's first General Assembly was held in 1908, the second in 1911 and the third in 1914. In its early phase the Party was federalist in character, allowing represen-

tation from each of the country's historical territories, regardless of
the number of activists to be found there. This political agitation by
Nationalists went hand-in-hand with a cultural awakening which
took place during these years. In 1918 the *Sociedad de Estudios
Vascos* (The Society of Basque Studies) was born, later giving way
to the creation of the *Academia de la Lengua Vasca* (The Academy
of the Basque Language).

In 1923 the newly established dictatorship of Primo de Rivera
banned the activities of the more extreme branch of the Nationalist
Movement under the leadership of Eli Gallastegi, although it tolerated those of the more moderate branch. After the dictator's fall in
1930 these two branches came together and the pro-Republican Pact
of San Sebastián was signed, in the absence of representatives of the
Nationalist Party. This agreement gave birth to a second Nationalist
party, *Acción Nacionalista Vasca* (Basque Nationalist Action), more
secular and left-wing in character, while another group rallying
around the magazine *Yagi Yagi* was concerned with principles to do
with the country's independence.

At the municipal elections of 1931 the Republicans swept the
board and the King left Spain. The Carlists and the Basque Nationalists, united in their religious fervour and their defence of the ancient
rights which they enjoyed in common, put up coalition candidates at
the elections and emerged as winners. The mayor of Guetxo in
Vizcaya, namely José Antonio Agirre, called a meeting of the *Juntas
Generales* (General Assemblies) of that province with the intention
of proclaiming a Basque Republic, but the new Government in
Madrid used force to prevent this meeting from taking place.

The internal difficulties of the Carlist-Nationalist coalition,
which were encouraged by the Government in Madrid, prevented
the implementation of the Statute of Autonomy of Estella, which
would have united the four southern provinces. In its place a
scheme for only the three western provinces was put to a referendum on 5 November 1933, resulting in a poll in which 84% of the
electorate were in favour. In October 1935, at a meeting in San
Sebastián, the Spanish monarchist leader José Calvo Sotelo uttered
the famous phrase, ' A red Spain is preferable to a Spain torn
asunder'. In the following February, on the occasion of the legislative elections, the Popular Front won a victory in all parts of the
Spanish State. Franco's uprising in July 1936 led a few months
later, during the Civil War that followed and in an attempt to enlist
the support of Basque Nationalism, to the Republican
Government's acceptance of the Statute of Autonomy which had
been in abeyance since the referendum of 1933. José Antonio Agirre

was nominated President of the territory and the Statute was put into effect.

The Civil War, to which we shall return later, ended with the defeat of the Basque forces, both left-wing and Nationalist, and the establishment in Madrid of the Franco regime which lasted until the dictator's death in 1975. In 1945 the Basque Government, under the presidency of José Antonio Agirre, set itself up in New York. Finding its authority disputed by Republicans in exile, it carried on without further reference to them. The meeting of the Assembly of the Basque Nationalist Party held in Paris in 1950 was followed a little later by the expulsion of the Basque Government from its base in that city by order of the French Government.

The reader who wishes to have a summary of the Party's ideology during the years from 1956 to the death of Franco should read *La causa vasca*, the work of Javier Landaburu. Its contents tend to be openly Christian Democrat, European Federalist, and strongly in favour of the Basques' right to self-determination.

The Party's failure to act was so conspicous during the Franco years, however, particularly in the eyes of younger people, that it tried to compensate by organizing in 1956 the Basque World Congress, as propaganda for its cause. The President of the Basque Government, José Antonio Agirre, died in March 1960 and his place was taken by Jesús Mariá Leizaola, a conservative-minded intellectual who was completely lacking in drive and vision.

The Basque national day

Since 1932 the Basques have celebrated their national day, known as *Aberri Eguna*, the festival of all Nationalists who are active on behalf of their country. The day creates a bond between the various tendencies and provinces, and between the generations. It is a good example of Basque militancy of the peaceful kind and has shown no sign of losing support since its inception. It also reflects, under various guises, both the internal and external difficulties experienced by the Basque Nationalist Movement.

The first *Aberri Eguna* was held in Bilbao, the birthplace of Sabino Arana. Tens of thousands attended from all parts of the Basque Country, gathering in front of the house where the founder of the *PNV* had been born. The second, also held under the auspices of the Party, took place in San Sebastián in 1933, and chose as its theme the question of national minorities in Europe; once again it attracted many thousands of people, among them Edward Ammende, Secretary General of the Assembly of European Peoples.

The third, held in 1934 in Vitoria, was also attended by enormous crowds. The fourth, in the year following, was to have been in Pamplona but had to be postponed until the month of June on account of the political tension of the time. Then, at the very last moment, despite a protest by the Basque members in the Republican Government, it was banned outright. In the end, the Member for Navarra, Manuel Irujo, won permission for the day to be held on the last day of June, and again tens of thousands turned out. The occasion was therefore the first in a series to be banned by the authorities and the beginning of a period of repression aimed at preventing the Basques from celebrating their national day. In the year following, 1936, the *Aberri Eguna* did not take place at all, even though the Civil War was not to start until a few months later. From this time on, and particularly after the defeat of the Basque forces, the festival was formally banned by the Franco regime.

In 1947 the Basque Government in Exile called for the national day to be held in Bilbao and, on 6 April, several thousand people gathered in front of the church of Saint Anthony. Meanwhile, at San Sebastián, a broadcast on Spanish radio was interrupted with the words, 'Basques, today we are celebrating our national day. Tune in to *Radio Euskadi! Gora Euskadi Askatuta!* ('Long live a free Basque Country!), after which a few words from the President, José Antonio Agirre, were transmitted. The *Aberri Eguna* of 1960 coincided with the death of Agirre. The day was marked by the hoisting of Basque flags on Mount Urgull at San Sebastián, but several religious ceremonies were interrupted by violence on the part of the police.

The first national day of any great significance to be held after the Civil War took place in 1963. On 15 April a great gathering of militants celebrated their day near Itxassou around a branch taken from the tree at Guernica, thus inaugurating a tradition which, despite several setbacks, has continued to this day. It was memorable in this respect: a lieutenant-colonel in the Spanish Army, who was present as a spy, was recognized and submitted to an interrogation during which he received a number of blows. In the southern part of the country there was no large gathering but a new organization known as *Euskadi Ta Askatasuna* (*ETA*) distributed leaflets in several districts and painted its initials in the streets of Bilbao and Getxco.

Between 1964 and 1968 there were large demonstrations, which the police tried to prevent at all costs, in Guernica, Bergara, Vitoria, Pamplona, and San Sebastián. With the exception of the *Aberri Eguna* of 1966, all these manifestations were in response to calls from the *PNV* and *ETA*. The following year, the order was not to take to the streets but to stay at home. A few demonstrations took place, nevertheless. The most striking incident of this year was the death of two militants from Navarra, both members of the youth section of the *PNV*, who were killed by their own bomb. Over the next few years there were pilgrimages to various mountains. In the northern part of the country demonstrations were held wherever an opportunity presented itself. In 1974 the President of the Basque Government in Exile, Jesús Mariá Leizaola, turned up unexpectedly in Guernica during the celebration of the national day. Between 1975 and 1977, just before and after the death of Franco, the festivals held at Guernica, Pamplona and Vitoria were put down with force.

In 1978 the *Aberri Eguna* was held more openly and generally than in the previous years. All the political parties, both Basque and Spanish, with the exception of the two parties from the Spanish Right (*UCD* and *AP*), brought out huge numbers of their supporters in the four capitals of the southern parts of the country. It was the largest celebration that had been seen up to then. The placard placed at the head of the demonstration in San Sebastián, which was carried by several politicians, among them the Socialist leader José Mariá Benegas, called for the right of self-determination for the Basque Country. Next day the Madrid newspapers expressed their unease at the size and demands of this gathering.

In 1979 a huge number of demonstrators again took to the streets in several towns and cities, this time calling for an amnesty for political prisoners and those who had been driven into exile. In the year following, at Pamplona, a popular rallying-place for Basque militants, a number of people were hurt as a result of police brutality, including two Members of Parliament from the separatist coalition known as *Herri Batasuna*. Many people who were unable to get into the city decided to demonstrate instead at Vitoria and San Sebastián. The appeal made by the Nationalist Left made most impact that day. In the north many people took part in a demonstration at Saint Palais.

In 1981 the route of the demonstration planned by *Herri Batasuna* was blocked by the police who had encircled the town. Nevertheless, there were demonstrations at Mungia, Durango and Algorta, while the *PNV* gathered its supporters at the Exhibition being held in Bilbao, as well as at Estibalitz and Leitza, and the group known as *Euskadiko Ezkerra* brought out a handful of its members for a demonstration which the authorities allowed to take place in Guipúzcoa. Much the same thing happened in the year following: the police tolerated demonstrations by the more moderate Nationalists and put down those organized by the radicals. Beginning in

1983, however, the street demonstrations organized by *Herri Batasuna* in Pamplona were tolerated, up to 1991. The same militants organized the *Aberri Eguna* of 1992, in the two frontier towns of Fuenterrabia and Hendaye. In the following year it was held on the left bank of the estuary in Bilbao, in protest against the dismantling of the region's industries. A year later the *Aberri Eguna* returned to Pamplona.

Up to the present time the Basque National Day has continued to be celebrated by enormous crowds. Two of the three Nationalist groups prefer to gather their members indoors, but the most radical, *Herri Batasuna*, marks this day with street demonstrations calling for independence for the Basque Country.

The birth of ETA

The political party created by Sabino Arana towards the end of the 19th century has gone through several phases. It can be considered as a Christian Democratic organization of a conservative kind which protects the interests of a capitalist economy, drawing its support more from middle-aged voters than from young people and having a growing tendency towards regionalism in a Spanish context. Its inactivity during the Franco years led to the emergence in 1952 of another Nationalist group by the name of *Ekin* (Action), which was founded by a number of young people from Vizcaya and Guipúzcoa who wanted to make the Basque cause more dynamic.

Although the new group tried to win over the *PNV*, the staunchly negative attitude of certain of the latter's leaders prevented this from happening. The *PNV* was not prepared to give up its authority in Nationalist affairs, which was to prove inevitable later on, and in December 1958 the *Ekin* group changed its name to *Euskadi Ta Askatasuna* (The Basque Country and Liberty), or *ETA* for short.

The first attacks carried out in the name of *ETA* were explosions in the towns of Bilbao, Vitoria and Santander in 1959. Its most remarkable feat was the partly successful attempt, on 18 July 1961, to derail a train carrying Franco's supporters on their way to San Sebastián to celebrate the twenty-fifth anniversary of the outbreak of the Civil War. On the same day two Spanish flags were burnt in public at San Sebastián. The partial derailment of the train did not result in any deaths but the police took advantage of the sabotage to arrest and torture a number of suspects. In order to escape police brutality, a number of Basque militants fled to the northern part of the country where the first exiles of the post-war period had begun to congregate.

The first conference of *ETA*, which was held in 1962, took place for this reason in the north.The young organization now worked out its ideological basis, which of course reflected the new situation and the spirit of the decade in which these changes were taking place. Among the first things that *ETA* did were to denounce racism and replace it, as a priority, with an active defence of the Basque language; it also opposed the Christian Democratic ideology of the *PNV* with a radical secularism and a keen commitment to the cause of the working-class. With the advent of *ETA* Basque Nationalism became progressive. As for its military wing, it was at this time only in embryo.

In the same year a general strike was called in the provinces of Vizcaya and Guipúzcoa, and also in Asturias and eventually throughout the peninsula, thus causing the first state of emergency since Franco had seized power. In the north of the Basque Country the first measures by the French authorities against members of *ETA* took the form of house arrests.

It was at this time that a member of the Academy of the Basque Language, Federico Krutwig, exiled by the Franco regime, wrote his book *Vasconia*, a work of separatist ideology which took the side of the guerrillas and thus exerted a profound influence on the first generation of *ETA* militants. In the year following the group known as *Enbata* ('the strong wind from the sea which blows before a storm') was founded in the northern Basque Country. This organization blazed a new trail in the Basque struggle, its members gathering around a magazine of the same name which has survived to this day. The work carried out by *Enbata* proved essential not only in the encouragement of a Basque consciousness in the northern provinces but also as a means of enlisting public support for those Basque militants who took refuge there from the threat of reprisal.

Conferences of *ETA* were held regularly thereafter: the second in 1963, the third in 1964, the fourth in 1965 and the fifth between 1966 and 1967. Given the ferocity of the persecution carried out by agents of the Franco regime, it was possible to hold only the last two in the southern part of the country. The second conference did not reach an over-view of the Basque situation. The third gave its approval, in the Basque context, to the use of revolutionary military tactics. The fourth adopted Marxism as its ideology, arguing that the national problem and the social problem were but two aspects of the same reality. The fifth conference, which was held in two parts, worked out the organization's basic principles, which remained in place up to the death of Franco in 1975. It brought together the theories of national and social liberation, adopting the term 'the Basque working people' and creating four wings to be responsible for its activities in the cultural, political, working-class and military fields. The first part of the conference was devoted to the expulsion of those who were seeking to convert *ETA* into a workers' party with a Spanish dimension.

During the 1960s the influence of *ETA* and those associated with it, as well as that of the *PNV*, played an important part in the rapid renaissance of Basque culture and the gains made by the Basque language and the *ikastolak*. These private and clandestine schools teaching through the medium of the language, about which we have spoken in the preceding chapter, took enormous strides forward during the decade.

In the month of June 1968 the leader of the fifth conference, Txabi Etxebarrieta, a native of Bilbao, killed a policeman at a road-block. This was the first instance of a killing by *ETA*. A few hours later the police shot Etxebarrieta, who in turn became the first member of the new organization to die in action. Throughout the country there were strong protests at the shooting of the militant. The second killing by *ETA* took place in the following August when the police torturer Melitón Manzanas was gunned down on the doorstep of his home in Irun. By now it was clear that *ETA* had taken up arms. The Franco regime promptly declared a state of emergency in the province of Guipúzcoa. In the same year a group of about sixty priests occupied the seminary of Derio in Vizcaya, calling for the recognition of Basque rights and a more democratic Church. In 1969 the police arrested almost the entire directorate of *ETA* and, as we have seen, on *Aberri Eguna* two young members of the *PNV* died when a bomb they were carrying exploded prematurely. The following year, at Saint-Jean-de-Luz (known in Basque as Donibane Lohitzun), the association *Anai Artea* (Between Brothers) was formed to help political refugees now coming up in increasing numbers from the southern parts of the Basque Country. At the sixth conference of *ETA*, held in September 1970, there was an attempt to form a workers' party with a Spanish dimension but this was prevented by a number of leading members from *ETA*'s old guard.

Following a series of demonstrations and arrests, in December 1970, the military trial of sixteen *ETA* members took place at Burgos. Six of them, accused of causing the death of the policeman Manzanas, were condemned to death. This trial was marked by the largest demonstrations ever seen in the Basque Country and it had strong repercussions, even beyond the country's borders. All kinds of organizations opposed to the Franco regime, both Basque and Spanish, took the Basque side in this confrontation. The protests led to a general strike and the kidnapping by *ETA* of the German Consul at San Sebastián.

A short while after the verdict was delivered a new state of emergency was declared in the province of Guipúzcoa. The sentence, announced at the end of December, condemned the six main defendants to death, imposing on two of them a double death-sentence. The uproar which followed was such that, on the last day of the year, the dictator Franco was obliged publicly to grant the accused a reprieve.

What came to be known as 'the Burgos trials' were important for two reasons: they served as a sounding-board for the Basque cause and a medium of propaganda for *ETA*.

The year 1973 was an outstanding one for *ETA*, not only because the first part of its sixth conference was held then but also because it killed Admiral Luis Carrero Blanco, Franco's second-in-command and President of the Spanish Government. Because of the way it was carried out, by the use of a car-bomb, and the repercussions it caused, this was generally considered to be the most spectacular act by *ETA* up to that time.

Towards the end of the year following there was a split between the so-called 'political-military' and the 'military' wings of *ETA*. The first of these was in favour of dividing the organization into two distinct parts: the one a political directorate and the other, under its jurisdiction, having a military function. The 'military' wing was in favour of a single organization of a military nature. There was a complete schism between these two irreconcilable camps. In the same year, throughout the Basque Country, a sensational general strike was held against the Franco regime and, in the year following, three more strikes in protest against the regime's oppression. The 'political-military' wing of *ETA* held a number of conferences: at the beginning of 1975 (the second part of the sixth conference which had not been officially drawn to a close), the seventh in September 1976, and the eighth and last in February 1982. At its seventh conference it decided to launch a legal political party, which took the name *Partido para la Revolución Vasca* (Party of the Basque Revolution), known thereafter by its Basque initials of *EIA*.

The 'political-military' wing was wound up a few years later, so that the present *ETA* is properly considered as the successor to what was called at the time the 'military' wing. The deaths of its three leaders define the history of *ETA* over the four decades of its existence: that of Txabi Etxebarrieta, who was killed by police in 1968, that of José Miguel Beñeran, known as Argala, also killed by undercover police in 1978, and that of Txomin Iturbe, who died in an accident in Algiers in 1987. The armed campaign of *ETA* has exerted a powerful influence on the course of Basque politics. The organization has caused many deaths and injuries, and a great deal of damage to property, and many of its own members have fallen in the armed struggle. Its actions have been directed mainly against the police and the Spanish Army, and those who collaborate with them, as well as against drug-dealers and those involved in the building of the nuclear power-station at Lemoiz.

It should be noted that *ETA* has never been in favour of indiscriminate terrorism, by which is meant random attacks, but has always chosen its targets carefully. In an interview broadcast by the German television station *West-3* on 12 April 1994, *ETA* made the following statement: 'Our struggle has always been and continues to be selective. If we use a booby-trapped car, it is to strike against our enemies, those who oppress our people, and no one else. On the other hand, while we are aware that there have been mistakes in recent years, the victims were not deliberately chosen. The way we operate does not and will not allow that. There have been blunders and errors and we have given much thought to preventing them from happening again. We try to use methods that will not result in the death of innocent people, for our sole targets are those who oppress the Basque people.'

The serious mistakes committed by *ETA* over the years have no doubt discredited the organization to some extent. On the other hand, the fact that it has admitted and given an account of them has brought it credibility in the eyes of the Basque public, which always knows whether an incident should be attributed to it or not. The influence of *ETA* on Basque society, however, cannot be measured only in terms of its armed campaign and the direct and indirect consequences that flow from it. The social policies of *ETA* since the 1960s have given it considerable influence in various sectors of Basque life, such as politics, culture, festivals, international relations, the language, and in others which we cannot go into here.

Three referenda during a period of transition

The last executions to be carried out by the Franco regime, which took place in September 1975, provoked lively protest in the Basque Country. Two Basque militants were among those who stood trial. Seven of the nine members of the European Community recalled their ambassadors from Madrid. The regime responded by declaring one last state of emergency in Guipúzcoa and Vizcaya and organizing a Fascist demonstration on the Plaza de Oriente in Madrid which was led by Franco and his successor, Prince Juan Carlos. But in the month following the dictator was to die.

The Regency Council then proclaimed Juan Carlos Chief of State. He was chosen by Franco himself, the man who had brushed aside Don Juan de Bourbon, the father of the new king and heir to the dynasty. The official proclamation ended with these words: 'In loving remembrance of Franco, long live the King!'.

These events gave birth to the *Coordinadora Patriota Socialista* (Coalition of Socialist Patriots), known by its Basque initials *KAS*, which had come into existence for the protection of militants whose lives were in danger. This new grouping brought together the two wings of *ETA* as well as various other radical Nationalists, their main aim being to co-ordinate the struggle against the executions of September 1975.

In view of its ability to mobilize people of different persuasions, *KAS* now decided to establish itself on a permanent basis. During the course of 1976 it set out a programme which contained eight points, and these were reduced to five in the following January. This programme, known as the *KAS* alternative, which is summarized later in this chapter, defined the minimum conditions under which *ETA* would be prepared to give up the armed struggle and the Nationalist Left to participate in the country's institutional life. The *KAS*, which is very much alive to this day and serves as an intermediary between those who carry on the armed struggle and those who work in other ways, was remodelled in 1983 following publication of a report entitled *KAS, bloque dirigente*. In 1976, the year of the drawing up of 'the *KAS* alternative', the campaign spread throughout the Basque Country, causing no fewer than three general strikes in that year and two more in the year following.

In order gradually to prepare for the inevitable transition from the Franco regime to a more tolerant system, the Government proposed on 15 December 1976 a referendum on political reform. All parties belonging to what was called 'the Opposition', including the *PSOE* (*Partido Socialista Obreros España*), the *PCE* (*Partido Communista de España*) and the *UCD* (*Union de Centro Democratico*), as well as all the Basque parties, called on their supporters to abstain. The actual rate of abstention by Opposition parties throughout Spain, only 22.6% of the electorate, was probably attributable to widespread intimidation by the Government and the lack of opportunity for the expression of support for other options. In the four southern provinces of the Basque Country the rate of abstention was much higher, although it did not constitute a majority: it was 42.8%.

At the end of 1977 the flying of the Basque flag, banned up to now, was once again allowed.

We should note here, because of their impact on the formation of Basque public opinion, the founding of two new daily newspapers which now joined those which had existed before the advent of Franco: *Deia* (The Call) in Vizcaya, launched by the *PNV* in June 1977, and *Egin* (To Do), first published by the Nationalist Left in September of the same year. These two papers still have a wide circulation, despite several Government threats to stop the publication of the latter.

In the month of June 1977 there were elections to the *Cortes* (Parliament) in Madrid, in which nearly all political parties could take part. The *PSOE* and the *PNV* won most of the votes cast in the southern Basque Country and there was a weak showing by candidates from the Nationalist Left, mainly because most of its supporters opted for abstention in protest against the Government's refusal to grant an amnesty for political prisoners. Four days after the Election, 28 of the 42 M.P.s and Senators who had just been elected to seats in the southern provinces gathered under the symbolic tree at Guernica to express their support for Basque autonomy, the legalization of all political parties, without exception, and an amnesty for all prisoners.

The elected members taking part in this meeting were the M.P.s of the *PNV* and the *PSOE* representing the four Basque provinces, together with one from the small party known as the *ESEI* and a number from the Spanish Right (*UCD*) who had been elected in Vizcaya. There were three parliamentarians from Navarra: two M.P.s from the *PSOE* and a Senator from the *PNV*. The contribution made by the representative from the *UCD* set the tone of the meeting: 'We are firmly of the opinion that there should exist in the Basque Country, in the near future, a base of political power, to be exercised from somewhere within the country, possibly Pamplona.'

The meeting made it clear that, before taking their seats in the *Cortes*, the elected representatives would elicit the opinion of the Basque people. Despite several more meetings, this attempt to provide the four provinces with an autonomous and united voice was thwarted by Madrid, as has happened on every occasion when a way has been sought for the realization of Basque aspirations. This setback was something of a milestone and provided clear proof of the unanimity demonstrated by the Basque people at this moment in their history. The experiment also showed how effective a united approach could be for the four provinces, instead of the separate initiatives which usually keep them apart. A short while after this

first election, there was a 'Freedom March' throughout the length
and breadth of the Basque Country, calling for democracy, autonomy and an amnesty for prisoners and exiles.

The next phase of the transition to democracy was the referendum
on the new Spanish Constitution held on 6 December 1978. In
keeping with monarchical tradition, there was no consultation on
this issue. For the whole of Spain the response in favour was only
59% of the electorate; in the Basque Country, however, this attempt
at assimilation suffered a clear setback, for the Basques refused to
approve a legal text which did not recognize their identity. Indeed,
the 'yes' vote on the proposed Constitution was only 34.9% of the
electorate. It must be borne in mind that all the Basque parties had
advocated abstention and that the Spanish parties, including those
on the Left, had been in favour. The 'yes' vote was composed of
42.3% of the electorate in Álava, 27.7% in Guipúzcoa, 50.4% in
Navarra, and 31.1% in Vizcaya, which came to a meagre 'yes' vote
of 34.9%. Just as the Madrid Government had foreseen, the Constitution could not count on the approval of the Basques, thanks to the
opposition of the country's political parties. This rejection on the
part of the Basques is a key to understanding the instability of their
country and the conflicts which now rend it.

We should note here that the first demonstration by the *PNV*
against *ETA* took place at this time, on 28 October 1978, a month
before the referendum on the Constitution. During this demonstration, which had an important effect on the development of the
Basque cause and on the country's political life, a flight of white
doves was released, for which reason it was known as 'the demonstration of the doves'.

The third referendum which marked the transition to democracy
was organized a year later, on 25 October 1979. It sought approval
for a Statute of Autonomy for the three western provinces of the
Basque Country, the so-called *vascongadas*, but excluding Navarra.
The Statute which was now put to the vote was not the one worked
out at Vitoria and Guernica by the parties which were in favour of
self-government, but a watered-down version which had the approval of Madrid. The exclusion of Navarra from the terms of the
referendum showed that the Government expected a certain answer.
There was only one question and it referred to the area in which the
proposed Statute was to apply.

The unity of Navarra and the three other provinces has always
been and continues to be of great importance in the Basque argument. The matter should have been resolved at this point in the
transition process, for practically all the parties at this time — the

Nationalists, the Navarra parties, and the main Spanish parties —
were in agreement about the unification of the four provinces under
a single Statute with Pamplona as capital of the whole territory. This
position is maintained today only by the Nationalists, for by now
there exists a clear difference of opinion in Navarra, which compli-
cates the issue and makes a solution much more difficult.

The importance of the affair within the Basque movement was
underlined by these words of Xavier Arzalluz, the President of the
PNV, in March 1986: '*ETA* would lay down its arms immediately if
Navarra became part of Euskadi.' This politician has several times
put his finger on the sore by stating that the unity of the southern
provinces has been thwarted by direct pressure from the Spanish
Army on the Madrid Government, in order to prevent the Basque
Country from becoming economically prosperous and territorially
integrated, which in Madrid's view would be tantamount to running
the risk of secession. It was therefore not the wish of the people
directly concerned, nor even that of the Navarrese, which decided at
this time that the Basque Country should remain disunited, but
rather forces outside the country.

In describing the years from 1977 to 1980 as a period of transition,
we should note that it was not only the Nationalist parties but also
those of the Spanish Left which were in favour of the unification of
the four Basque provinces; even the right-wing in Navarra was in
favour, albeit less so. The Basque sections of the *PCE* and the *PSOE*
included, at this time, all four provinces. Later, after armed force had
brought about their separation, these two parties reorganized their
membership in two sections, one comprising the three western provinces and the other a Navarrese section.

As proof of its support for integration, we can offer this sentence
from a statement made by the Basque section of the *PCE* on 5 August
1977: 'We are in favour of the integration of Navarra into the Basque
Country for reasons that are cultural, economic, and in particular,
political.' That the local leaders of the *PSOE* were also in favour of
the integration of Navarra is clear from a statement by one of them,
José Mariá Benegas, on 19 August 1977: 'The crux of the matter lies
in finding a formula which is acceptable to both parties, so that
Navarra neither remains on the periphery nor is completely integrated into the Basque Country, and this should be a temporary
measure while we await a Statute for all four Basque provinces.
Navarra is part of the Basque Country and as such it should be
integrated into the scheme which is to bring autonomy to the country.' Two months later, on 22 October 1977, Benegas said: 'The
attitude of the *UCD* Government towards the inclusion of Navarra

as part of the Basque Country is now more favourable. Following the re-establishment of the Foral Congress of Navarra earlier in the year, it can now be integrated with the other Basque provinces.' The Socialist leader Gabriel Urralburu, from Navarra, deplored the difference of opinion on the Basque question within the right-wing Spanish party, the *UCD*, on 8 January 1978: ' The *UCD* wants to prevent any sort of link between Navarra and the Basque Country.' His colleague, V.M. Arbeloa, was reported as saying on 24 May 1980: 'There is one question which both preoccupies and excites us; it is that regarding the link between Navarra and the rest of the Basque Country.' Yet these two parties on the Spanish Left, the *PCE* and the *PSOE*, would later later split over the question.

During this period of transition the right-wing parties of Navarra would also look favourably on the case for the integration of the province. Its spokesman Jaime Ignacio del Burgo said on 5 November 1977: 'As a native of Navarra, I love everything Basque. We are inclined to facilitate the inclusion of the province under the terms of the Statute of Autonomy.' Although the main right-wing party in Navarra, now called the *UPN* (*Union del Pueblo Navarro*), had within it a nucleus of members who were opposed to Basque integration, some of its leaders were in favour, such as its President, Juan Cruz Alli, who declared on 18 September 1991: ' The Autonomous Communities of the Basque Country and Navarra can no longer ignore each other as they have done up to now. I consider myself Navarrese and as such I can renounce neither my Basque roots nor my Basque names.'

But let us leave this long digression about the territorial integrity of the Basque Country which has been shattered by the Statute of Autonomy. Before we do so, however, we should not forget that the organizers of the referendum of 1979, since it was held in only three out of the four provinces, knew full well what the response was likely to be. We should also examine the circumstances under which the referendum was held.

During the run-up to the referendum, the authorities had distributed large numbers of a booklet entitled *12 Minutes con el Estatuto* (12 Minutes with the Statute), which — under the pretence of summarizing the text — actually outlined a much more acceptable Statute than the one that was on offer. The statements made in favour of the Statute reflected this embellishment, this distortion of the real text. Here, for example, is what Mario Onaindia, one of the Statute's supporters, said on 23 February 1979: 'The Statute represents the Basque people's most sincere aspirations, both democratic and national, summed up in the phrase "*que se vayan*"; it re-establishes the "Economic Agreements", it offers a democratic plan for the Basque language, and with regard to the integration of Navarra, it reverses what was being proposed by the *UCD*.' Now that water has gone under the bridge, we have to point out that, on the contrary, the popular slogan *'que se vayan'* ('let them leave'), which means that the Spanish police should leave the Basque Country, has not been realized, given that the National Police and the Civil Guard still exist; that the Basque language is still optional while Spanish is compulsory; and that Navarra still has to be integrated with the other provinces. The only point among those made by Mario Onainda which has come about is the one about the re-establishment of the 'Economic Agreements', that is to say control over the tax-system.

There was also talk, after the acceptance of the Statute, that political prisoners would be released from gaol, but this was only further dressing up of the Statute's real content, in order to win votes. Furthermore, there were some serious irregularities at the time of the referendum. The *UCD*, which was the main advocate of the 'yes' vote, hardly played any part in the campaign, in order to remove all Spanish opposition to the proposed Statute. The number of people on the electoral register dwindled from day to day. The postal vote was carried out in conditions which would have been unimaginable in any other European country: in some areas the dead voted, people who were not on the electoral register were allowed to cast their votes, some had more than one vote, and so on.

Under these conditions it was no wonder that the 'yes' vote won a majority of 53.1% of the electorate. Feeble though it was, the result was enough to allow the Statute to be put into effect at the Palace of Moncloa in Madrid on 17 July 1979, when it was signed by the President of the Spanish State and the President of the *PNV*. This was the Statute which brought about the division of the southern Basque Country into two parts — the western provinces (the *CAV*) on the one hand and Navarra on the other; it also confirmed the inferiority of the Basque language in law and made it impossible to exercise the right of self-determination.

It should be borne in mind that at the referendum of 1976 all the democratic parties, both Basque and Spanish, had recommended abstention and that at the constitutional referendum of 1978 only the Basques had continued to take this position. At the third referendum, however, only the most radical of the Basque parties, namely *Herri Batasuna*, took this line, for the reason that the proposed Statute was setting out only administrative decentralization and not the granting of real political power, or territorial integrity for the Basque Country, or any degree of equality for the language. The 'yes' vote of 53% can be compared with the 84% of voters who gave their assent on 5 November 1933, in the days of the Republic. The difference between these two percentages is a measure of the popular support for the statutory proposal at these two moments in Basque history. If the scheme put to referendum in 1979 had included the clauses of what was known as 'the *KAS* alternative', which gave a degree of recognition and political power to the southern Basque Country and also corresponded roughly to what the people wanted, there is reason to believe that the percentage of 'yes' votes would have been similar to what it had been in 1933. But the Spanish Government categorically refused to allow the inclusion in the Statute of those clauses for which the people had expressed support.

Limited though they were, these three referenda of 1976, 1978 and 1979 determined the institutional structure of the Spanish State in the years following the end of the Franco regime, including that of the southern Basque Country. The way in which they were put to the people, and subsequent events, were to reveal how inadequate they were for solving the problems which still remained.

The institutional separation of the western Basque provinces (*CAV*) from that of Navarra, established in 1979, was to be confirmed by the law known as the *Amejoramiento del Fuero Navarro* (Improvement of Foral Rights in Navarra) which was passed in 1982 without being put to a referendum. It is also significant that the Spanish Constitution states in article 145 that 'in no instance will the federation of the Communities be allowed. The first elections for the Parliament of the *CAV*, held in March 1980, led to the formation of the first Autonomous Government of this part of the Basque Country. A few years later an Autonomous Government was set up in Navarra.

The final stages of the transition from the Franco regime to the present cannot be understood without reference to the coup d'état which was attempted in the *Cortes* on 23 February 1981 with the compliance of certain senior Army officers. Indeed, the reasons given for this rebellion were the protests which had recently taken place in the Basque Country. These included the interruption by a group of *Herri Batasuna* leaders of a speech by the King in Guernica, the killing by *ETA* of one of the directors of the nuclear power-station at Lemoiz, and a general strike called in protest at the death under police torture of a Basque militant. Furthermore, the coup d'état ended as a result of an agreement between those who had provoked it and those who had suffered from it. This agreement was drawn up under the infamous law known as the *Ley Orgánica de Armonización del Proceso Autonómico* (Organic Law of Harmonization of the

Process of Autonomy), or *LOAPA*, which was approved by the *Cortes* on 30 June 1982. By coincidence, or perhaps deliberately, it was approved on the same day as the *Ley de Amejoramiento del Fuero Navarro*, by which the southern Basque Country was divided, also became law.

The unexplained disappearance of the Conservative party, the *UCD*, which had formed the Government since the beginning of the transition period (there is no parallel anywhere in Europe for its demise) led to the coming to power of the *PSOE* in October 1982, the date on which the transitional period may be considered to have come to an end.

The creation of Herri Batasuna

After the first elections since the end of the Franco regime in June 1977, a number of small parties on the Nationalist Left which had been opposed to participation began to come together with a view to creating a new party which would represent their political aspirations. The first instance of co-operation between these groups took place in October 1977, although the new alignment would not come into formal existence until a year later when twelve people well-known in the political field joined to form *Herri Batasuna*, which means 'Unity of the People'.

Herri Batasuna is more a coalition, a movement or a political formation than a political party proper. It brings together people of diverse ideologies who are in agreement on a common programme. Nevertheless, and only after it had overcome numerous obstacles placed in its way by Socialists in the Ministry of the Interior, it was made a legal political party in June 1986. Its political programme is 'the *KAS* alternative', which we have already mentioned, and it includes the following five points: an amnesty for political prisoners and refugees; the legalization of those parties which want independence from Spain; the withdrawal of the Spanish police force; an economy which instead of being run by an oligarchy would protect the interests of the working-class; and a new Statute of Autonomy for the four southern provinces which would include the right to self-determination, control of the armed forces, the recognition of Basque sovereignty, and the rapid development of the Basque language.

We reproduce 'the *KAS* alternative' in detail here not only for ease of reference but also because it has been an important part of the Basque case from 1976 to the present. The version given here is that of 1978 which has not substantially changed since it was first drafted.

1 Amnesty: the release of all Basque political prisoners.
2 Democratic rights: the legalization of all political parties seeking Basque independence without any reduction in their status.
3 The expulsion from the Basque Country of the Civil Guard, the Armed Police and the General Police Corps.
4 The improvement of living and working conditions for the common people and the working class in particular.
5 A Statute of Autonomy which fulfils the following minimum conditions:
   * its simultaneous application to all four historic regions of the southern Basque Country
   *recognition of the national sovereignty of the Basque Country and the right to self-determination, including the right to form an independent State
   *recognition of the national links that exist between the north and south of the Basque Country
   *the Basque language to be official and to have priority
   *the civil defence forces replacing the present oppressive forces to be created by the Basque Government and to be answerable to it alone
   *the armed forces garrisoned in the southern Basque Country to be under the control of the Basque Government
   *the Basque people to have sufficient powers to allow it always to have economic structures which it deems to be best suited, in social and political terms, to its progress and well-being.

This political programme is advocated as much by *ETA* as by *Herri Batasuna* and its implementation would depend, as far as the former is concerned, on an end to the armed struggle, and for the latter, its regular participation in the country's institutional life. The elected representatives of *Herri Batasuna* carry out their function as members of the Municipal Councils but, except on special occasions, they do not attend the *Cortes* in Madrid. Nor do they take their seats in the two Autonomous Parliaments in Vitoria and Pamplona, nor in the *Juntas Generales* of the western provinces of the *CAV*, demonstrating by their absence that they do not recognize the democratic legitimacy of those institutions. Leaving aside for a moment the long-term implications of the programme, both *ETA* and the rest of the *Coordinara KAS* and *Herri Batasuna* campaign for a Basque Country of which the general characteristics would be political independence, a democratic system allowing the participation of all its citizens, the territorial unity of the country, and the normalization of its language.

To complete our summary of *Herri Batasuna*'s programme, it should be added that it published its own plan for a Statute of

Autonomy in December 1978 and another in June 1990. The latter, revised and then published, is known as the National Statute of Autonomy; it includes all four of the southern provinces, rejects the two other Statutes already in existence and supports 'the *KAS* alternative'.

The appearance of *Herri Batasuna* on the political stage coincided with a moment of great excitement in the public life of the Basque Country. As an example, let us take the general strike which was held throughout the southern provinces in July 1978 in protest against violent attacks by the police during the festival at San Fermín. In the year following there were three more strikes: one in protest against the death of a militant ecologist killed by the Civil Guard, the second against the death of a demonstrator, again at the hands of the police, and the third against what is known as the *Estatuto de los Trabajadores* (Statute of Workers). As for the electoral struggle, the first confrontation which the new coalition had to face was the referendum on the Spanish Constitution held in December 1978, to which (as we have already seen) all the Basque parties were opposed, and which was rejected by the southern provinces.

The first elections in which *Herri Batasuna* took part were those held in March 1979 — the second round of legislative elections, the first having taken place in 1977. On this occasion the vote polled for the new party was so high that it was the main surprise on voting day. Out of a total of 1,900,000 votes cast in the four provinces, the *PNV* won with 290,000 votes, followed by the *PSOE* with 245,000, and then *Herri Batasuna* with 172,000. There were further upsets in store. At the first municipal elections, held just a month later, the outcome was spectacularly different. *Herri Batasuna* now won 222,000 votes, this time beating the *PSOE* and thus becoming the second force in the southern Basque Country. The second surprise was the dazzling success of the *PNV*, which picked up 366,000 votes. How was it that 76,000 voters who had not voted for the *PNV* in March came to do so a month later? Apart from the fact that the confrontation at municipal level gave the party a relative advantage, the reason for this surprise result could only have been the strength of *Herri Batasuna* in the elections of March 1979. It seems that some conservative-minded voters thought like this: the only way to protect ourselves against the growth of a Nationalist party which is separatist is to vote for a conservative party which is just as Nationalist, rather than vote for any of the Spanish Conservative parties.

This rather simplistic way of thinking may explain to a large extent one of the most significant aspects of Basque political life in recent years: the beginning of a return to power by the *PNV* in April

1979, which was to continue thereafter. The comeback of this party which had received only a mediocre vote at the legislative elections of 1977 and an even worse one in 1979, was confirmed in the month following. We are persuaded that this improvement in the showing of the *PNV* was caused by the intervention of *Herri Batasuna*.

To return to *Herri Batasuna*, we should note that it has received a fairly stable vote since the first electoral contests of 1979 and that this has been so right up to the present. It has won seats in the *Cortes* and in the Autonomous Parliaments, and many of its members are mayors and councillors on the Municipal Councils. We have already noted that, although it sometimes wins seats, *Herri Batasuna* participates only in municipal affairs and does not attend meetings of any Parliament, in order not to compromise its integrity. After the legislative and municipal elections of 1979, in October of that year, *Herri Batasuna* found itself alone in opposing the Statute of Autonomy for the three western provinces (*CAV*), of which we have already spoken, and it was partly responsible for the poor 'yes' vote of 53.1%.

From that point on *Herri Batasuna* has taken part in all the usual elections, as well as in the referendum on Spain's membership of NATO, with which we shall deal later. The movement also plays a prominent part in other areas such as the organizing of demonstrations, support for the Basque language, the protection of the environment, and the denunciation of corruption.

Chapter 4

A DECADE OF SCHISM

In this rapid account of the Basque question and of officialdom's refusal to recognize it, we have already referred to the way in which the Franco regime was reformed, and we have now reached the legislative elections of 1982 which brought the *PSOE* to power in Madrid. One of the most significant events which occurred in the Basque Country after the return of the Socialists was doubtless the split in the most important of the Basque political parties, namely the *PNV*.

The split in the PNV

Throughout the history of the Basque Nationalist Party there have been differences of opinion between the Nationalist wing and the Regionalist, and this tension has contributed to schism within its ranks. The most recent example was the expulsion of the party's branch in Bermeo in Vizcaya, which happened in 1980. Those who were expelled were known as *'los sabinianos'* on account of their doctrinal allegiance to the founder of Basque Nationalism, Sabino Arana. But the most serious schism took place a few years later, in 1986.

In May 1984 most of the leading active members of the *PNV* in Navarra were expelled for not carrying out an order to lend their support to the Spanish Right in the province; the order applied to an area much bigger than Navarra. As a result of these differences, the President of the Vitoria Government, Carlos Garaikoetxea, was sacked and replaced by José Antonio Ardanza. Early in January 1985, when there was mounting tension within the *PNV* in Navarra, the party's conference in Guipuzcoa withdrew its support for the office in the province and replaced it with another which was more critical of the leadership. In the same month a new Government was elected in Vitoria, made up of members from the *PSOE* and a weakened *PNV*, following a *Pacto de Legislatura* (Legislative Pact).

In the course of 1986 a network of bugging devices was discovered that the *PNV*, which had just expelled its branches in Vitoria, had used to spy on the ex-President, Garaikoetxea. A short while afterwards, in September of the same year, the schism in the *PNV* took place and a new group, *Eusko Alkartasuna* (Basque Solidarity), which had been expelled by the *PNV*, came into existence. The provincial office of Guipúzcoa and the *PNV* in Navarra joined this new group, causing serious altercations about the ownership of various local premises. Because many members of the Parliament of Vitoria declared themselves in favour of the new party, it became necessary to bring forward the elections to this autonomous body to November 1986.

The name by which the media referred to the two opposing wings varied as the months went by. At first they spoke of 'the party machine' against 'the Parliamentarians', then of 'the foralists' against 'the Vitoria centralists', then of 'the officialists' against 'the critics', and finally of the *PNV* against *EA*. The crisis virtually split the *PNV* into two halves: both the leadership and the membership were divided. In electoral terms the consequences for the Party, which had been in a majority up to now, were very serious. Whereas it had received 470,000 votes at the elections for the Autonomous Parliaments in February 1984, it polled only 310,000 votes in the legislative elections of June 1986. At the elections for the Autonomous Parliaments, which had been brought forward to November 1986, the breakaway group put up candidates using its own initials *EA*. The results were as follows: 276,000 votes for the *PNV* and 181,000 for *EA*. But at the next elections, the gap between them narrowed: the *PNV* now lost votes, polling only 237,000, while *EA* increased its share, polling 210,000. This near-balance would be shattered, however, in 1989 when the *PNV* began to make a steady recovery. Nevertheless, the repercussions of the split within the *PNV* were not without their significance in electoral terms and they played an important part in remodelling its leadership.

The differences of opinion which were brought to light during this crisis within the *PNV* had their roots in the years 1983 and 1984, at the time when the *Ley de Territorios Historicos* (Historical Territories Law) was under discussion: the official camp favoured giving more power to each of the three provinces while the dissident faction (the future *EA*) preferred reinforcing the Government in Vitoria. The subsequent divergence arose out of a demand by the leadership of the *PNV* in Navarra that support should be given to the Spanish Right, to which the Party strongly objected. Another cause of contention arose

in March 1986 on the occasion of the referendum on Spain's joining
NATO, for the leaders of the *PNV* had announced that they would
vote in favour while those in Navarra were against. The official wing
also accused the leader of the dissidents, Garaikoetxea, of surrounding himself with young people of a Social Democratic persuasion who
were not fully under the control of the Party's leaders. The various
leaders of the official camp made numerous statements against full
independence while the dissidents declared themselves in favour. On
the other hand, however, the main leader of the dissidents objected to
including independence among the new party's aims. Although this
decision did not please everyone, it was nevertheless accepted. It
should be added that *EA*'s purview took in the whole of the Basque
Country, north and south, while that of the *PNV* has always been
confined to the southern parts; it was not until later that it created a
token section in the northern provinces.

After the elections for the Autonomous Parliament in November
1986, the long wait while the Government of Vitoria was formed
threw into relief another difference of opinion between the two
parties, which by now had completely separated. Whenever the two
discussed conditions for a coalition with the *PSOE*, the PNV would
not demand the transference of Social Security to the Government
in Vitoria, whereas *EA* always did. For this reason the Spanish party
preferred to ally itself with the *PNV*, the less demanding of the two.
The first European Elections of June 1987 brought yet another
difference out into the open: the *PNV* was seen to be the international
ally of Christian Democrat parties, whereas *EA* chose to co-operate
with Green and Nationalist groups.

We have spoken thus far of the clear differences between the two
factions of conservative Nationalism. However, the deeper reasons
which separated them seem to have been connected with the Statute
of the *CAV*, which was now revealed to be a further obstacle. Indeed,
at the time of the referendum on the Statute, in October 1979, the
Basques were divided into two camps: one had no confidence in this
Statute and therefore abstained from voting, while the other, with an
eye to the future, supported it as the lesser of two evils, though
without much trust in it. As a consequence of the implementation of
this text by the Government in Madrid, the endless delays in the
transfer of powers, the cancelling by the Spanish capital of numerous agreements drawn up in Vitoria, and particularly the interminable discussions and difficulties attendant upon each and every
stage of this process, a good many of those who had supported the
Statute at the outset now expressed their disappointment at the way
it was being implemented.

Furthermore, the two camps within the population of the *CAV* now became three, and this situation may be considered to have continued up to the present: those who had voted for the Statute and were still satisfied with it, those who had not supported it and still do not support it, and lastly, those who had hesitated at the time of the referendum but now found themselves disappointed by its application. This factor must be borne in mind if the present situation in the Basque Country is to be properly understood. We propose illustrating all this with some quotations, although we cannot represent all the various points of view held by so many on the political stage.

The newspaper *La Gaceta Ilustrada* on 1 January 1981 published an interview with the President of the *PNV*, Xavier Arzalluz, who was reported as saying: 'What is happening is that in Madrid there is so little political acumen that sometimes they are unable to take any action, while the others [meaning *ETA*] are as active as bees in a hive. That's what is so terrible. I just don't understand it. At the end of the day, who can justify violence? *ETA*'s problem is a political one, because without the popular support on which it still relies it would be nothing. In Madrid they ought to understand that, thanks to us, and the fact that we agreed to negotiate the Statute, thus running some serious risks, it has proved possible to turn the political-military wing of *ETA* in the direction of negotiation. And after we have accomplished that, they fling the *Ley Orgánica de Armonización del Proceso de Autonómico*, the *LOAPA*, at us, which could wreck everything that's been built up to the present. It's unbelievable.'

Although the *PNV* is, with the *PSOE*, one of the parties which are most satisfied with the Statute of Autonomy as it is now being implemented, some of the things its President has said suggest a relative dissatisfaction, as when he declared on 8 November 1980: 'The federalism of North America is more advanced than the Statute of Guernica.'

Our next quotation is from Mario Onaindia, one of those condemned to death at the Burgos trials, today a member of the *PSOE*, and at the time of the following declaration a leader of a moderate party belonging to the Nationalist Left: 'If Basque society does not enjoy at the moment a sufficient degree of normalization, and if there is not on the central Government's part a recognition of what has been approved by the Basque people, by what right are we to tell *ETA*: but why do you talk about self-determination when there has been a referendum which has approved a Statute of Autonomy? For these same *ETA* militants read every day the declarations of the Basque Government, which are true, to the effect that the Spanish

Government is not in the process of transferring powers and that it does not respect the Statute of Autonomy.'

For his part, Carlos Garaikoetxea, the President of *EA*, has taken the same line on several occasions, expressing his growing discontent, not about the Statute of Autonomy as it now exists in the *CAV*, but about the deplorable way in which it has been implemented by Madrid. Here are a few quotations from certain of his disciples which express this frustration. J.J. Pujana said on 17 January 1988: 'We wouldn't accept the Statute now.'

J.Elosegi recalled on 17 April 1988: 'We had many illusions regarding the Statute of Guernica.' As for J. Azkarraga, he declared on 15 February 1989: 'The only thing that can possibly be done to the Statute of Guernica is reform it.'

To sum up, this question of the Statute's failure to satisfy the Basque desire for sovereignty is no doubt at the root of the *PNV*'s division into two factions, on one side those who have chosen a more Regionalist path (the *PNV*) and, on the other, those who take a more Nationalist line (*EA*).

We cannot conclude this chapter without going back for a moment to the constitution of the new Government at Vitoria following the elections to the Autonomous Parliament of November 1986, for there occurred at this time a surprising incident which should not be left out of our account, although it is not quite relevant to the question of schism within the *PNV*.

On 26 February 1987 the Parliament of Vitoria was the setting for an event the like of which had never before seen in Europe: a Basque political prisoner delivered a speech to the Chamber on behalf of *Herri Batasuna* and as a candidate for the Presidency of the Autonomous Government. The parliamentary session was taken up with the formation of the new Government following the elections of 30 June 1986. Outside the building an enormous crowd had gathered, which despite police harassment was able to hear the speech by means of loudspeakers. This unusual candidate was Juan Carlos Yoldi, aged 24, a metal-worker, who was a political prisoner on remand from Herrera de la Mancha and awaiting his sentence for having been a member of *ETA*. He had been brought from his cell and was now, under constant police surveillance, addressing the Parliament. Facing him was the other candidate for the Presidency, José Antonio Ardanza, who was to be elected by the 17 votes of his party, the *PNV*, the 19 votes of the *PSOE* and the two from the *CDS*, a Spanish Centre party, which accounted for 38 of the 75 votes. As for *EA*, *EE* (a moderate leftist group) and *CP* (on the Spanish Right), they abstained. Ardanza presented a programme which was designed, he said, 'to ensure that Euskadi in 1990 will be a peaceful society'.

The young prisoner read his speech with self-assurance and conviction. At the end of the two speeches and during the debate on the election of the President, the *Herri Batasuna* members walked out of the Parliament, 'in the belief that this institution is not valid and does not represent the interests of the Basque people.'

As for Yoldi, when asked on his way out of the building what he had been feeling while he read his speech, he replied: 'Whenever I looked at Ardanza, the members of the *PSOE*, the *EA* members and Garaikoetxea, I felt real pity for them. I thought to myself, if those are the people who are going to be in charge of our affairs and lead our people, then we are badly served.' In the same year, in July, a similar scene took place in the Foral Parliament of Navarra when during the session that was about to choose the new President of the Government, the political prisoner Guillermo Arbeloa, accused like Yoldi of belonging to *ETA*, addressed the gathering on behalf of *Herri Batasuna*.

A new phase in the north

Although the greater part of our account refers to the southern part of the Basque Country, the more heavily populated and industrialized, the northern part also has a national movement, which though cautious at first has grown steadily over the years.

The Nationalist group *Aintzina* (Forward), to which the writers Pierres Lafitte and Marc Legasse belonged, was active in the 1930s and during the Second World War. Once the war was over, in 1945, when the French National Assembly was working on the text of its new Constitution, Marc Legasse drafted a scheme for a Statute of Autonomy for this part of the country, within the context of the Fourth Republic. The Basque M.P. Jean Etcheverry-Aintchart presented the plan to the working party on the Constitution and, although the proposal was not accepted, it bore witness to the existence of a nucleus of Basque Nationalists in the northern provinces.

Marc Legasse, who for many years edited the satirical-political magazine *Hordago,* was imprisoned and fined many times on account of his political activities. He took part in a number of elections, representing various Nationalist groups, and also in hunger-strikes in support of refugees from the south.

The Nationalist group subsequently created in the north of the country, was called *Embata* ('the strong wind from the sea which blows before a storm'), about which we have already spoken, and during the 1950s it was made up of students from the Basque Country who were living in Bordeaux, Paris and Toulouse. This new movement, independent of all other Nationalist organizations, published from September 1960 a magazine called *Enbata* (the letter 'n' adopted from the new Basque orthography).

In 1963 *Enbata* was formally constituted and played a prominent part in organizing at Itsasu (Itxasu) in Labourd the first *Aberri Eguna* to be held since the Civil War. The meeting at Itxasu ended with the reading and approval of a Charter that was to serve as a basis for the coming together of Nationalists in the north. The event was attended by representatives of Nationalist groups from elsewhere in Europe who, by their presence, contributed to the importance of the national day.

Here are some extracts from the Itxasu Charter:

> 'The Basque nation is at present divided into two parts, under the jurisdiction of the French and Spanish States. The Basque language is on the way to extinction. The economy of the three northern provinces is in recession, emptying them of their population, especially their young people.

> 'The various current French theories about political, economic and cultural reorganization, whether in the context of the French State or in that of the new Europe, do not take into consideration the real interests of the Basque Country.

> 'That being so, *Enbata*, assembled on 15 April 1963 at Itxasu in Labourd, proposes to the Basque people:

> 'In the first place, and while respecting the Constitution and laws that govern the French Republic, the creation of a Basque *département* to include the three provinces of Soule, Basse Navarre and Labourd, one which would be run in accordance with a Basque language statute.

> 'Secondly, and within the European Union, the formation of an autonomous political, administrative and cultural region which would reunite the seven Basque provinces and be in federation with the other European regions.'

From 1970 on, the activities of the *Enbata* group became limited to publishing its magazine, the holding of hunger-strikes and standing trial on charges brought against it by the French authorities. The magazine was published without interruption until 30 January 1974, on which date the French Council of Ministers banned the organization. However, the magazine resumed publication about a year later.

From 1967 *Enbata* also put up candidates at various elections, and this initiative was followed by other Nationalist groups which emerged in the north of the country.

For an understanding of the electoral history of the northern Basque Country only the legislative elections and, more recently, those of the so-called 'regionals' (the Regional Parliament at Bordeaux) are relevant, for various technical reasons that we need not go into here. The Nationalists first put up candidates in the northern provinces at the legislative elections of March 1967, at which *Enbata* polled 4.6% of the vote. In June 1968, however, their share of the vote went down to 1.6%. In 1978 the Nationalist party which contested the elections was called *Euskal Herriko Abertzale Sozialistak* and it received 3.6% of the vote. In 1986 it was *Ezkerreko Mugimendu Abertzalea* (Nationalist Movement of the Left), founded in the previous year, which put up candidates, polling 3.7%.

At the next legislative elections, in 1988, the Nationalist candidates received 5.1% of the vote. At the regional elections of 1992 two of the Nationalist groups, using the initials *EMA*, of which we have already spoken, together with *Euskal Batasuna* (Basque Unity), founded in 1986, put up coalition candidates who between them received 7.2%. In addition, a third Nationalist group, *Eusko Alkartasuna*, belonging to the party of the same name in the south which had split from the *PNV*, as we mentioned earlier, received 1.1% of the vote. So the Nationalist vote on this occasion amounted to 8.3% of the votes cast, the highest percentage ever received.

At the legislative elections of 1993 the coalition of *EMA* and *EB* won 5.4% of the vote and *Eusko Alkartasuna* 1.1%, a total of 6.5%. In short, we can speak of a weak showing by these parties, but with both highs and lows, and in general a slight tendency to increase from election to election.

In the northern Basque Country there has been a remarkable disparity between a weak Nationalist presence at the political level and much greater activity in such areas of social life as economic planning, sport, culture and action on behalf of the Basque language. At the same time, the most important new development of the last few decades has been the emergence of armed groups, notably that of *Iparretarrak* (Those from the North), which have had a considerable influence on political life.

On 11 December 1973 *Iparretarrak* carried out its first attack in the vicinity of Banca in Basse Navarre, as part of a campaign connected with industrial conflict at a medical centre. This group was very much under the influence of the Nationalist Movement and the armed struggle in the south, and this raid preceded, by just a few

days, the blowing up of Carrero Blanco. The inaugural number of
its magazine *Ildo* (Furrow) came out in 1974 and it was not until the
end of 1977 that its first member was arrested. For a long time the
presence of those engaged in armed struggle in the north of the
country was the subject of much controversy, but eventually, despite
strong initial opposition, it was accepted by the majority of Nationalist groups.

Between 1978 and 1981 another armed group came into being
which went by the name of *Hordago*. Early in 1980 two members of
Iparretarrek died while preparing to go on a raid and several others
later lost their lives in action.

Over the years there have been numerous armed attacks by
Iparretarrak, notably against tourist installations, public buildings,
policemen, informers, and employment agencies. Its voice has also
been raised in defence of the environment. The group has never
pretended that it is in favour of insurrection but it has always been
outspoken in denouncing the apparatus of the French State. In 1983
a policeman was killed and a member of *Iparretarrak* lost his life
during a confrontation between militants and the French police. In
July 1987 the group was banned by the French Government. In
February of the year following, Philippe Bidart was arrested on
suspicion of being the leader of the armed faction.

The campaign of *Iparretarrak* has been carried on with growing
momentum in recent years and, as we have already noted, it has been
more and more accepted by the various Nationalist groups of the
northern Basque Country. In 1994 an important rapprochement
occurred between *Herri Batasuna* and the three main Nationalist
groups in the north, namely *Ezkerro Mugimendu Abertzalea, Euskal
Batasuna* and *Herriaren Alde* (In Favour of the People).

Electoral panorama

We have just been looking at the electoral situation in the northern
Basque Country. Let us now turn to the corresponding scene in the
south. We shall conclude with an assessment of the Nationalist vote
for the whole of the Basque Country.

Of the 2,200,000 voters on the electoral register of the southern
Basque Country, there are usually between 600,000 and 1,000,000
who abstain. The votes are shared between the eight principal par-
ties, of which three are Spanish, three Basque and two provincial.
The first group includes the *PSOE* (a Social Democratic party), the
Partido Popular (a Conservative party), and *Izquierda Unida* (a
Communist party). The second group consists of the *PNV, Eusko*

Alkartasuna and *Herri Batasuna.* Of the two provincial parties the more important is the *Unión del Pueblo Navarra* (Union of the Navarrese People); the other is the *Unidad Alavesa* (Union of Alava). Between 1977 and 1993 there also existed another party, *Euskadiko Ezkerra,* but most of its members have now joined the *PSOE,* the rest going over to the other Nationalist parties.

The largest parties in the south of the Basque Country are the *PSOE,* the *PP* and the *PNV,* each polling about 300,000 votes. After them come *Herri Batasuna* with about 200,000 votes, *EA* with 120,000, and the *UPN* with 70,000. The weakest parties are the *IU* and *UA.* The Basque parties and the provincial parties usually poll better at local elections than at General Elections. This is particularly true of the *PNV,* the *UPN* and *UA* and less true of *Herri Batasuna* and *EA.* As for the Spanish parties, the opposite is generally true: they poll better at the legislative elections, that is to say those for the Assemblies in Madrid. Furthermore, the number of votes cast in the Basque Country for the Spanish parties tend to go up or down just as they do in the rest of Spain. The *PSOE* lost votes in the first legislative elections held after the end of the Franco regime in 1977. On the other hand, in 1982 there was a spectacular increase in its vote which was comparable with what it polled in the rest of the Spanish State. For all that, it has more recently lost support which it did not regain until the legislative elections of 1993, at which it recovered a large number of votes in the four Basque provinces, once again thanks to a closely fought electoral battle (reflected throughout the State) with the parties of the traditional Spanish Right. The opposite happened at the European Elections of June 1994, again a phenomenon that was determined by Madrid. Much the same happened in the legislative elections held on 3 March 1996, when a struggle between the *PSOE* and the *PP* was won by the latter. As for the distribution of votes in the four provinces, the *PSOE* and *Herri Batasuna* have fairly even support throughout the Basque Country while the *PNV* is weak in Navarra. Relatively speaking, the *PSOE* is strong in Álava, *Herri Batasuna* in Guipúzcoa, the *UPN* in Navarra and the *PNV* in Vizcaya.

The fact that there are no fewer than eight parties is a reflection of a society which has serious contradictions which remain unresolved and institutions which are inadequate and in need of change.The large number of parties and the small share of votes polled by each of them are characteristic of the electoral fragmentation of the southern Basque Country and the source of many institutional problems which are sometimes of a very complicated nature.

The primary explanation for the large number of political parties lies in the confrontation between the Right-Left axis and the Basque-Spanish axis. As for the similar number of votes cast for the various parties and the absence of any one dominant party, these have their origins in the splitting of the *PNV* into two parties in 1986. The consequence of all this is that each institution requires a different coalition, thus making for an instability that is endemic. The framework is very complex and unpredictable. For decisions to be taken that will be to the benefit of the Basque people a more solid base and longer timescales will have to be made possible.

Of the Autonomous Governments, the one in Vitoria (the *CAV*) is usually run by a coalition of the *PNV* and the *PSOE*, while the Autonomous Government of Navarra is in the hands of the *PSOE* and the *UPN*.

Although the strength of the Nationalist vote throughout the country, north and south, varies from one election to the next, we shall give for reference the results of the Regional Elections of 1992 for the north and those of the provincial *Juntas* of 1991 for the south.

In the Regional Elections for the Parliament at Bordeaux, which were held on 22 March 1992, the two Nationalist candidates polled between them a total of 8.3% of the votes cast. The remaining 91.7% were shared among French parties such as the *UDF* (*Union et Democratie Française*), the *RPR* (*Rassemblement pour la Republique*), the *PSF* (*Parti Socialiste Français*), the *PCF* (*Parti Communiste Français*), and so on, as well as other groups involved in specific issues like hunting, employment, and the environment. The vast majority of the inhabitants of the northern Basque Country therefore feel themselves to be French, at least when it comes to voting.

In the south, at the elections for the Provincial *Juntas* and the Foral Parliament of Navarra, held on 26 May 1991, there were four Basque parties: the *PNV, Herri Batasuna, EA* and *EE.* The total number of votes cast for these four parties amounted to 49.8% in Álava, 72.4% in Guipúzcoa, 19.8% in Navarra, and 65.2% in Vizcaya. The rest of the votes went to Spanish parties such as the *PSOE,* the *PP* and *IU* (*Izquerida Unida*), or else to provincial Spanish parties like the *UPN* (*Unión del Pueblo Navarro*) in Navarra or the *UA* (*Unidad Alavesa*) in Álava.

To sum up, the Nationalist vote amounted to 8.3% of the electorate in the northern Basque Country and 55.8% in the south. This gives an average of 51.7% for Basque Nationalist parties and 48.3% for French and Spanish parties. Although this is no doubt an over-simplified view, it appears that the Nationalist vote in the Basque Country amounts to a slight majority.

As for the southern Basque Country, in those elections which took place for the Provincial Parliaments between 1991 and 1996 the percentage of the vote for Spanish parties has been increasing and that for Basque parties decreasing.

In order to put these statistics into their social context, if only superficially, we should note here that the Basque population can at present be divided into three parts, according to its geographical origins: about one third was born outside the Basque Country, another third inside the country of Basque stock, and another third inside the country of immigrant parents.

Attempts at negotiation

According to radical Nationalists, the tension between the Spanish State and the Basque Country cannot be resolved by force, which would mean the annihilation of one side or the other, but only by means of political negotiation. This point of view has been shared, albeit in a somewhat inconsistent fashion, by others. Be that as it may, it seems clear from opinion polls that the Basques are broadly in favour of a negotiated solution at the earliest possible moment.

Although the Spanish Government has sometimes admitted it and at other times denied it, the fact is that it has made contact with *ETA* with a view to negotiation on numerous occasions. In 1975, immediately after the death of Franco, meetings took place between a representative of the new King (the future Minister Marcelino Oreja) and representatives of the military wing of *ETA*. The first meeting was held in Bayonne with Txomin Iturbe as intermediary and the second in Biarritz, in the presence of the latter and of José Miguel Beñaran, who was to die in an attack in 1978. The King's representative tried to obtain a truce from *ETA* in exchange for a few promises, but *ETA* took the view that the proposal was neither clear nor definite enough.

Following the passing of the *Ley de la Reforma Política* (Law of Political Reform) other initiatives were taken in Geneva between representatives of the political-military wing of *ETA* and three senior officers of the Spanish Army. The latter offered the release of prisoners, the repatriation of exiles, and the legalization of political parties in exchange for an *ETA* ceasefire lasting three months. At a second meeting in Geneva, early in 1977, two representatives of the military wing of *ETA* were present. They made it clear that they would not negotiate with the Government while the legalization of political parties had not been put into effect. On the other hand, the political-military wing continued to maintain their contacts in Paris and, some while later, with the Spanish State. Later the same year, representatives of the political-military wing of *ETA* had meetings in Spain with several members of the Spanish Army and police with a view to obtaining freedom of movement for prisoners and exiles. Members of the *KAS* also kept up contacts with a representative of the Army.

In 1978 Josep Tarradellas, President of the *Generalitat* of Catalonia, and Jesús María Leizaola, President of the Basque Government, still in exile, met (at the request of the head of the Madrid Government, Adolfo Suárez) two leaders of the military wing of *ETA*, one of whom was Txomin Iturbe, to look into the feasibility of a ceasefire. The meeting took place in the vicinity of Le Boulou, in northern Catalonia, a few kilometres from the border. In the same year other attempts were made to open up a dialogue. In June the journalist José María Portell served as a go-between for the Ministry of the Interior and *ETA*. Iñaki Esnaola, a defence lawyer for *ETA* prisoners, former Mayor of Deba and the Civil Governor of Guipúzcoa, also initiated a series of talks. Later still in 1978, the Minister of the Interior, Rodolfo Martín Villa, offered to hold a meeting with *ETA* anywhere in Europe. Although the Minister travelled as far as Switzerland, the meeting did not take place because *ETA* insisted on contact being made in public.

On 15 May 1978 Felipe González announced in the Bilbao newspaper *Hoja del Lunes:* 'With all the responsibility that this implies in political terms, I can say that I am in favour of negotiating with *ETA*.' Another attempt at negotiation took place in this same year. This time the chief participant was José María Benegas, one of the top men in the *PSOE*, at the time in opposition, who made the following statement: '*ETA* is unable to accept as a mediator someone who plays a protagonist's role in this affair. I believe that if the two parties are to agree to negotiation, it must be direct.' Benegas then tried to meet the leader of *ETA*, José Miguel Beñaran, at St. Jean de Luz, but the latter, believing there were no guarantees connected with this initiative, refused to meet him.

On 11 May 1980 it was the turn of José María de Areilza, the Conservative leader, to announce that he was in favour of negotiation with *ETA*. In 1981 the Minister of the Interior, Juan José Rosón, opened a dialogue with representatives of the political-military wing of *ETA* and reached agreement on a ceasefire as a preliminary condition for the release of prisoners and the repatriation of several hundred refugees, a move which would lead to the demise of the political-military wing.

A few years later, in February 1984, Enrique Rodríguez Galindo, the Commander of the Civil Guard, met Txomin Iturbe in a café in Andorra but the meeting ended without reaching agreement. During the course of the following months two members of *CESID* (*Centro Superior de Investigación de la Defensa*, the Spanish Army Intelligence Service), who claimed to represent the Government, met Iturbe, first in France and then in the Belgian village of Mons and then in Lausanne in Switzerland.

In July 1984 Felipe González, now in Government, tried another way and called José María Martín Patino, a Jesuit, to the Palace of Moncloa. The latter had played an important role in the Episcopal Conference during the period of transition from the Franco years. The Jesuit, with a companion, met Iturbe in Paris but, despite the cordial tone of their long meeting, this attempt also failed because *ETA* would allow only a dialogue on political lines.

On 22 August of that same year the Socialist Minister of the Interior, José Barrionuevo, announced that he was ready to meet Txomin Iturbe 'wherever and whenever he wishes'. *ETA*'s reply was that 'the *KAS* alternative' could be the only basis for negotiation. Then, in September, Pierre Guidoni, the French Ambassador in Madrid, held a meeting, with the approval of Felipe González, with two leaders of *Herri Batasuna*, in order to inform them of his country's readiness not to proceed with the extradition of Basque refugees if *ETA* would accept a truce, but this was taken by *ETA* to be no more than a threat.

At the beginning of 1985, Major Rodríguez Galindo contacted Kepa Ordoki, a former Basque general during the Spanish Civil War and the Second World War, with the intention of seeking a meeting with *ETA*, but the latter preferred not to respond to this invitation because it seemed to be too closely linked with the police. From now on it would be the Army that would have to do the negotiating. Indeed, in October of the same year, the Basque industrialist Juan Félix Eriz claimed that, during the summer, he had been contacted by *CESID* and that he had been asked to sound out *ETA* with a view to negotiation. A month later, representatives of the police and Army were claiming that, since August, they had been having contact with members of *ETA* in Geneva, Andorra and Brussels. On 15 October 1985 the former Minister of the Interior, Juan José Rosón (*UCD*), argued in favour of negotiation with *ETA* 'with no tricks involved'. According to reports in the media, the Spanish Government, for four months in 1986, maintained contact with Txomin Iturbe up to his deportation to Algiers in July.

The talks in Algiers

In 1986 several talks were held in Algiers between Txomin Iturbe and representatives of the Spanish State. At the first round, in November 1986, the Minister of the Interior was represented by a police prosecutor and the conversation was strained. At the second meeting, in January 1987, which involved three senior civil servants from the Ministry, Iturbe demanded the transfer to Algiers of his comrade Eugenio Etxebeste. The following month Iturbe was killed in an accident. His burial in his native village of Mondragón in Guipúzcoa on 8 March 1987 was witnessed by an enormous crowd in one of the most moving manifestations of popular support ever given to *ETA*.

On 19 June 1987 *ETA* carried out an attack on the Hipercor supermarket in Barcelona, causing the death of twenty-one people and injuring many more. The police had received several warnings that a powerful bomb had been planted in the supermarket but preferred to do nothing about them, allowing the bomb to explode in order to discredit *ETA*. The verdict of the National Inquiry, published on 20 May 1994, recognized that if the police had responded as might have been expected during the hour between the militants' first warning and the explosion, the deaths would have been avoided. The consequence was that the State had to compensate the families of the victims. This gruesome attack, for which *ETA* would later reprimand its own members, caused a great deal of public commotion and prompted the Government's decision to send Eugenio Etxebeste, the *ETA* leader who had been deported to Ecuador, to Algiers with a view to reopening the discussions which had been interrupted by the death of Iturbe.

Up to now, two political observers have made a link between the Hipercor explosion and the resumption of talks in Algiers. The first is the American Robert Clark, an expert on *ETA* who has managed to get hold of information from the Spanish Ministry of the Interior. In his book *Negotiating with ETA*, published in 1990, he notes: 'Following the Hipercor bomb, the Spanish rapidly took a decision to renew the dialogue and on 10 or 11 July Etxebeste left Ecuador for Algeria.' The second observer is the spokesman for the Ministry of the Interior, Alberto Pozas, author of the book *Las Conversaciones secretas Gobierno-ETA*, which was published in 1992. He writes: 'Following the Hipercor attack it was decided to transfer Eugenio Etxebeste to Algeria in order to continue the search for a dialogue. The reaction to the attack opened up the possibility for politicians to denounce the criminal strategy of the terrorists and restart a process of dialogue in Algiers. Etxebeste arrived in Algiers in July 1987, this time on orders from Spain.'The first contact between Government representatives, on this occasion two police officers, and Eugenio Etxebeste took place on 11 August 1987 in a very tense atmosphere. The second occurred a month later. Between these two contacts, at the time of their meeting on 25 August 1987 in the Landes, the French President François Mitterand advised Felipe González to negotiate with *ETA* in order to solve the Basque problem. Next day, a *PNV* leader, Jesús Intxausti, was reported as saying that the possibility of talks was a very positive piece of news. Two days later, the Government spokesman Javier Solana surprised everyone by stating on television that: 'There always have been contacts with *ETA*, there are at present and there will be more in future.' At the second meeting, on 18 September, Etxebeste stressed the importance of having at the talks an intermediary who was not a police officer, if the way was to be opened for a framework of political dialogue which had a chance of success.

These contacts were a prelude to the biggest offensive against Basque refugees which had been seen up to then on French territory. The Paris Government carried out a huge police operation on 3 October in which a large number of arrests were made and refugees were handed over by one police force to another. The whole operation was seen as a threat to the talks in Algiers. The former President of the *PNV*, Jesús Intxausti, interviewed by the daily newspaper *Egin* on 15 November 1987, commented: 'I myself have always understood the *ETA* problem, from whatever angle you look at it, to be a political problem, and so the solution too must be political. I am convinced that without negotiation the solution will be difficult or that, even worse, it will have no solution at all. Thinking that it might be solved by repressive means, by police methods, is tantamount to madness.'In the following October and November more meetings were held with Etxebeste, this time for the discussion of political matters, but now it was a politician, one of the leaders of the *PSOE,* who represented the Spanish party. On the same day as one of these meetings, the second-in-command of the *FLN* (*Front de Libération Nationale*, the Algerian independence movement) left for Madrid where he had talks with Felipe González. So it was at this time that an anti-*ETA* pact was signed, to which almost all the political parties, both Spanish and Basque, lent their support. The first signing of this pact took place in November 1987 in Madrid. All the Spanish parties, plus the Catalan *CIU* (*Convergencia i Unio*) and the Basque parties, the *PNV* and *EE*, added their signatures to a document which became known as 'the Madrid Pact'.

After a grisly raid by *ETA* on 11 December 1987 against a

barracks belonging to the Civil Guard in Zaragoza, the Spanish Government informed *ETA* that all contact would be suspended until it accepted a truce.

The so-called Madrid Pact was to be the precursor of two other pacts formulated in the southern Basque Country. The Ajuria Enea Pact (so called after the seat of the Basque Government), was signed on 12 January 1988 at Vitoria by the same parties together with *EA*, although the latter had some reservations which it presented in writing. A little later, on 7 October, these same parties, with the exception of the *PNV* and *EA*, plus a few smaller parties of a local character, signed a similar document at Pamplona.

On 27 January 1988 *ETA* publicly announced the possibility of a 60-day strike, which would be called off only if police hostilities ceased during this period, and in the context of talks which were then in progress in Algiers. This proposal for a bilateral truce received no response from the Spanish Government, but several statements leaked by the latter to the press, suggested that *ETA* had already agreed to a truce. This tendentious interpretation was put about so widely that *ETA* was obliged to publish a statement denying it, adding that without a preliminary meeting between the two sides there could be no truce. The Government chose not to respond and, at the end of February, *ETA* kidnapped a well-known industrialist in Madrid, Emiliano Revilla, holding him for eight months. During this time the Government put off all attempts at negotiation. One of the *Herri Batasuna* leaders who had several times been Mayor of Bergera then complained about the official failure to respond to *ETA*'s proposal: 'The proposal made in January is the most serious that this armed organization has ever made and it is deplorable that it has been interpreted as a sign of weakness, because it has knocked on the head the notion that it was conceived among our own people.'At the Ministry of the Interior José Barrionuevo was succeeded in July 1988 by José Luis Corcuera, but his main assistant in the Algiers talks, Rafael Vera, was kept on in this capacity. The day after his appointment Corcuera left secretly for Algiers.

Similarly, within the Government at Vitoria, the Interior Adviser was dismissed and his successor was reported as saying: 'I am in favour of negotiation with *ETA*. In life one often has to negotiate and, of course, we aren't going to refuse our people the means of negotiating.'After releasing the industrialist Revilla, on 30 October, *ETA* published another statement which was very similar to that of 27 January, and in which it repeated its intention of calling a bilateral truce lasting sixty days in order to open up talks with the Spanish Government. More than two months went by before the proposal took effect. In fact, after the great general strike of 14 December which was held throughout Spain in protest against the Government's economic policies, and not long after the publication in *Diario 16* of a long interview with *ETA*, during which the latter renewed its offer of negotiation, the Government conveyed to the armed organization a proposal which stipulated that, in exchange for a unilateral ceasefire lasting two weeks, it would be prepared to enter into discussions. It also guaranteed that these discussions would lead to a more meaningful dialogue than at previous meetings.

ETA accepted the proposal and replied on 7 January 1989 by declaring a unilateral ceasefire lasting a fortnight. Four days later, while the strike was still on, the French police arrested two *ETA* leaders in the northern Basque Country. After the fortnight had elapsed, the organization once again informed the public of a meeting which had taken place in Algiers between representatives of the Spanish Government and Eugenio Etxebeste, 'and which signals a positive development regarding the treatment of certain topics which have been practically not for discussion up to the present.''Following this meeting,' the communiqué went on, ' we have agreed to a timetable of political discussions in order to prepare for an exchange of views on various questions which have a bearing on the present conflict.' To this end agreement had been reached on the shape of further talks in Algiers: those taking part would be advisers to whom both sides would have access and the role of the mediator from the Algerian Government would be to take part in the conversations and in the compromises which would result from them. *ETA* also announced a bilateral strike lasting two months and beginning on 26 March, the national day.

The nine clauses of the communiqué were ratified by both sides and it was agreed that it would be *ETA* which would announce them. It was also agreed that the Government, in order to avoid any explicit involvement, would confine itself to sending out another communiqué, a briefer and less definite one, approving in broad outline that of *ETA*. A few hours after the release of the *ETA* statement, the Government put out one of its own along the same lines.

Basque public opinion received the news about a bilateral strike with optimism because it seemed to open the way towards a lasting peace. The strike held and, between 15 January and 4 April, there were no more attacks by *ETA* and no further arrests by the police, which confirmed beyond the shadow of a doubt the bilateral character of this truce. In their editions for 30 January the magazines *Tiempo* and *Tribuna* published the results of an opinion poll which showed that a majority of the Basque population was in favour of negotiation. On 31 January the police union also declared itself in favour of 'political talks'.

Between 25 January and 22 March the two delegations met five times. The Spanish side was represented by the Socialist leaders Juan Manuel Eguiagaray and Rafael Vera, and the Basque side by Eugenio Etxebeste and two other militants, a woman and a man. The meetings were also attended by a general in the Algerian Army. The meat of the discussions consisted of how to reform the legacy of the Franco regime and its implications for the Basque Country. On 4 February the Vice-President of the *UPN*, a Navarrese party, stated: '*ETA* and the Government can now put political questions on the negotiating table, as long as these do not flout the law. The *KAS* alternative includes clauses which can easily be modified in negotiation and the implementation of some of them will not be a threat to the legal system now in operation.'The French judge Michel Legrand was quoted in the magazine *Cambio 16* on 16 February as saying, 'The police and the judiciary will not be able to resolve the problem of *ETA*.' Three days later, on 19 February, the President of the Government in Vitoria, having described himself as 'moderately optimistic' about the talks in Algiers, said, 'Now that these talks have failed, there's a good chance that the next round will take place in Belgium.'Throughout the process of negotiation the Minister of the Interior, José Luis Corcuera, several times called together the parties which had signed the Madrid Pact, in order to keep them abreast of developments and ensure their co-operation. The policeman and journalist Alberto Pozas made the point that 'the attitude which strikes Corcuera hardest is that of the leader of the main party in opposition, namely Manuel Fraga'. The latter, he said, not only accepted that the attempt at negotiation should continue but that he 'went further, offering to bring them about personally.' On 27 March, the day on which the two-month strike was due to end, and at about the time of the *Aberri Eguna*, *ETA* released a new eight-point communiqué in which it gave a summary of the meetings which had been held with the Spanish delegation and announced a second round of talks in Algiers. This initiative, said the communiqué, 'represents a new opportunity for discussion and real progress in the search for a negotiated settlement of the present confrontation.' Three other members of *ETA* would join the meetings and, parallel to these, another series of talks would take place between the *PSOE* and *Herri Batasuna*, before being opened up to other parties. The statement also announced that a new strike would begin, this time of three months' duration, ending on 24 June.

The eight points in the communiqué of 27 March, like the nine points of 23 January, had been worked out by the two sides during their talks, and it had once again been agreed that *ETA* would make the announcement and that the Spanish Government would, a few hours later, release its own confirmatory statement. However, the latter's response was confined to saying that the talks in Algiers had been positive. It went on to claim that it knew nothing about the contents of the *ETA* communiqué and, when it came to define the aim of the next round of talks, it replaced the phrase 'a negotiated political solution' with 'an agreed and definitive solution', making it understood that it was refusing to enter into political negotiation with *ETA*, despite having agreed to do so in Algiers. Furthermore, it insisted on defending the Constitution and Statute that were in force at the time, two of the principal causes of the discord. In all likelihood, it was as a result of pressure from outside that the Government did not dare to ratify the agreement reached with *ETA* on 27 March, and it was this backwards step which caused the talks in Algiers to be broken off.

ETA then put out a new communiqué in which it asked the Spanish Government to approve the eight points of the previous statement and made it clear that, if this were not done, the agreed clauses would be suspended and 'the struggle would start again on all fronts'. The Government refused and the explosion, on 8 April, of seven bombs in the State rail network and a letter-bomb at Irun, confirmed that the dialogue had come to an end.

Ten days later, on 18 April, the pressure exerted by Madrid on Algiers led to the deportation of six refugees from Algeria to Santa Dominica. Among them were the three people from *ETA* who had taken part in the talks with the Spanish Government. The over-riding influence of the latter on the Algerian Government had been felt from the outset but it had increased as a result of the political instability existing in North Africa at the time. It had also been reinforced by a series of favours which the Spanish Government had shown the Algerians: a slackening of its pro-Moroccan policies, the granting of large and cheap loans and even the release of an Algerian dissident who had been arrested in Spain.

A short while after the talks in Algiers, on 14 April 1989, a senior civil servant in the Basque Government, Luis Alberto Aramberri, stated that: 'The national aspirations of Basque society are not very different from what *ETA* argued for in Algiers.' On 5 May the French M.P. Nicole Pery, Vice-President of the European Parliament, said: 'France will continue to bring pressure to bear in favour of political negotiation.' In an interview given to *Egin* and published on 14 May 1989, the leader of *Izquierda Unida*, Julio Anguita, said:

'The talks were broken off because senior people made changes to what had already been agreed, from which we might draw the conclusion that those who took part in the talks in Algiers were merely messenger-boys.'The economist Ramón Tamanes, of the centre party *CDS* (*Centro Democratica y Social*), stated: 'Negotiation with *ETA* must continue here, or in Algiers, or somewhere else.'Two months after the talks in Algiers had ended, the political leaders of *ETA*, who were in prison, but who had been chosen to take part in the next round, gave their own interpretation: 'The Spanish delegation did not honour its commitment and disowned its representatives Vera and Eguiagaray. The weight of the most reactionary cadres was brought to bear in order to reach this conclusion, but the process is now irreversible and negotiation will have to be resumed sooner or later. . . The process started in Algiers is a *de facto* recognition of the ability of *ETA* to enter into dialogue and therefore all future initiatives must be at a higher level than those that have gone before.'Why did the Socialist Government take a step backwards from the agreement reached in Algiers by its two representatives? The reasons have never been made clear and we shall probably never know precisely what they were, because the Government was under heavy pressure on this score and the most confidential reasons were doubtless the most decisive, as usual. What is certain is that in 1989, following the two elections (the European and the legislatives), commentators in the Madrid press interpreted the Algiers agreement as a sign of weakness, even of treason. The Conservative newspaper *ABC*, on 29 March 1989, carried the headline, 'On the frontier of concessions'. The following day it said, 'Although *ETA* has been defeated by the police, the clumsiness of the Government has allowed it to win the political battle.'The daily paper *Ya*, also Conservative, commented on 30 March, 'We have been caught with our trousers down in Algiers.' Lastly, the daily left-wing paper *El Independiente* said on 5 April: 'Pressure from the Right forced the Government to alter the text agreed in Algiers.'The talks held in Algiers remain the most important attempt so far at negotiation made up to the present between *ETA* and the Spanish Government. Since the events of 1989 many contacts have taken place between the two protagonists with a view to eventually resuming negotiation, but not one has produced anything concrete. There have frequently been statements against negotiation between *ETA* and the Spanish Government, but also a few that have been in favour of resuming talks. For example, on 8 August 1990 Baltasar Marín, the chief of the Autonomous Basque Police, said: 'The Spanish Government and *ETA* cannot get out of having to negotiate with each other round the table, as in Algiers.'

Philippe Marchand, the French Minister of the Interior, also stated in an interview published in *El País* on 21 June 1991 that 'sooner or later there will have to be negotiations, for it is difficult to imagine a solution that is not political'.

The famous French writer Gilles Perrault, author of the novel *L'Orchestre Rouge* (1967), was among those who addressed a meeting of Basque refugees in the northern part of the country in November 1991. He ended his speech with these words: 'You know full well, you know better than anyone, that for the last fifty years, for the last hundred years, for several centuries now, in this cruel civil war that has been imposed upon you, what decides victory is never the number of soldiers, it is not financial power, it is not the importance of who is allied with whom . . . What counts is the will-power, determination. The winner is the one who resists for a little while longer, and I am confident that you will do just that . . . '

At the time of the *ETA* statement broadcast by the German channel *West-3* on 12 April 1994, from which we quoted in the previous chapter, the question put to *ETA* was: 'What would be the conditions under which the organization would agree to enter into negotiations like those in Algiers?' The answer was: 'The first condition is that they should be serious. The second is a genuine wish to resolve the conflict. And the third is a guarantee that this process will be pursued to its conclusion. We are not inclined to engage in yet another initiative if the conditions are going to be the same as before. This is what we are asking for: the will to bring this political conflict to an end and the necessary conditions for its solution. That is what we are asking for and what we need, and that is what we are laying down as a condition.'

Chapter 5

A STORY WITH A LONG HISTORY

Social phenomena are not produced by chance and the Basque conflict is a social phenomenon, one which has deep roots and a long history. From a brief account of the history of the Basque Country, the reader will gather that, over the centuries, the Basques have resolutely upheld their institutions, their laws and their customs. Although sometimes taking different forms, this tradition has been a constant feature.

In 778 on their way back from attacking the Saracens of Zaragoza and destroying the walls of the town of Pamplona, the troops of Charlemagne passed through the territory of what was to become the Kingdom of Navarra. It was for this reason that the Basques united to punish the mighty aggressor and his army, wiping out his rear-guard at Roncesvalles and killing Roland, the Emperor's lieutenant. The history of the Basques therefore begins with a huge popular rising against an aggressor. The epic poem *La Chanson de Roland*, the first work of any importance in French literature, wrongly attributes the attack at Roncesvalles to the Saracens, thus beginning a tradition that later official historians were to follow unquestioningly. In these accounts the Basque Country did not exist and, similarly, the historical facts would be turned upside down at the whim of each subsequent invading army.

The Kingdom of Navarra

It might be said, briefly, that in ancient times the Basques had good relations with the Romans, bad ones with the Goths, and good ones with the Arabs. In the chronicles of the Visigoth kings the note *'domuit vascones'* ('he conquered the Basques') appears time and time again, a reflection of the longstanding tension between them. The arrival of the Saracens in the Iberian peninsula, in the year 771, took the Vizigoth king Rodrigo by surprise just as he was about to lay siege to the town of Pamplona, which was the reason why he held the Basques responsible for his defeat at Guadelete.

The Kingdom of Pamplona was formed at the beginning of the 9th century and was known as the Kingdom of Pamplona and Najera towards the end of the 10th. It later became the Kingdom of Navarra, which kept its independence up to the beginning of the 16th century.

Although it had been one of the first Christian kingdoms in the Iberian peninsula, after the arrival of the Arabs, the Kingdom of Navarra soon lost its capacity for expansion and was overtaken by the Kingdoms of Aragón and Castilla, both of which were born, like the Castilian language itself, within the borders of Navarra at this time. After the decline of the Kingdom of Navarra and the simultaneous emergence of the Kingdom of Castilla, from the 12th to the 14th century, the western areas of the Basque Country, known today as the *provincias vascongadas*, considered an alliance with Castilla more attractive than one with Navarra. The subsequent union of Castilla and Aragón, brought about by the Catholic Kings, ushered in the conquest of Navarra in 1512 by the troops of the Duke of Alba, who with the connivance of Cardinal Cisneros expelled the Navarrese monarchs Catalina de Foix and Juan de Albret, the invasion winning moral support from the Papal bull, *Pastor Illae Caelestis.* We do not know whether this bull had been approved by the Spanish Kings or whether they had falsified it, but it excommunicated the Kings of Navarra and declared their Kingdom to be 'without legitimate monarchs', which meant that they would fall to the first invader.

During the course of the military occupation of the next ten years, there were several attempts to restore the independence of Navarra. The last took place in 1521, after which time the whole territory had been conquered. Having put down the *comuneros* of Villalar, the Spanish army concentrated its efforts on Navarra, crushing its forces and their allies on 30 June at the battle of Noain in which many thousands were killed. Among those who went on resisting in Navarra were several brothers of Saint François Xavier (Francisco Javier), who barricaded themselves inside the castle of Amaiur and held out until they were forced to surrender a year later. This castle, a symbol of the last resistance in Navarra, was then razed to the ground, like a number of others in the area. On account of the strategic position of Navarra, the army was to be permanently quartered there for the next several hundred years.

Three observations can be made about this late incorporation of Navarra into the territories under the Spanish Crown. First, there is a tendency to overlook the fact that Navarra was conquered by the Spanish later than a number of American territories. Secondly, the conquest meant only a change of dynasty, since Navarra continued to maintain its foral system with its own laws, its own borders, its own monetary system and its own *Cortes,* modelled on those of the other three provinces of the southern Basque Country, and these were to be the cause of permanent conflict in the long process of Spanish unification. Lastly, the conquest of Navarra by the Catholic Kings signalled the triumph of the Counter-Reformation, and the Inquisition, despite the extreme tolerance of the Court of Navarra itself. The Court was a model for cultural, religious and political tolerance throughout the 15th century in that part of Navarra not conquered by the Spanish. Under its protection literature and science flourished and the first books were printed in Basque. The *Cortes* of Navarra met for the last time in 1829, not long before the first Carlist War.

Assimilation of the northern Basque Country

About the year 1530, the northern Basques succeeded in defeating Castilian forces which, after the conquest, remained on their territory for only a few years more. In 1589 Henry III was made King of Navarre, following the fashion of his predecessors since the invasion, but he reigned over only the north Pyrenean part of the kingdom. After renouncing Protestantism and being converted to the Catholic faith, he was proclaimed King of France and Navarre, a title that was to be used by all the Kings of France up to the Revolution of 1789.

This king not only took Basse Navarre under the French Crown but also kept its identity intact as far as its administrative system and his right of succession were concerned. He also recognized the foral rights and native laws of his subjects, as did the Spanish kings in their part of Navarra. Under the Treaty of Vervins in 1598, Henry III gave up his claim to Spanish Navarra. We might say of the Kings of Spain and France that they could both legitimately call themselves 'King of Navarra', for one was effectively King of Navarra in the south and the other of Basse Navarre to the north.

Up to the Revolution of 1789 numerous attempts were made to undermine the legitimacy and sovereignty of the northern Basque Country but all were repulsed by its people: the suppression of 'witchcraft' in Labourd in 1609; attempts by the king to unite France and Navarra in 1616 and 1620; a move to suppress the States General of the Kingdom of Navarre in 1632; an insurrection in Labourd in

1657 against taxation imposed by Louis XIV; a rebellion in Soule in 1661 led by Matalaz; an uprising at Saint-Jean-de-Port in 1685 against encroachment on communal rights; and further uprisings against erosion of sovereignty between 1730 and 1776.

During the Revolution of 1789, the States General of the Kingdom of France invited the Parliament of Basse Navarre to participate in its affairs, but this invitation was turned down by the Parliament on the grounds that it 'constituted a distinct kingdom'. In the same year, the French National Assembly voted for the abolition of the constitutions of Basse Navarre, Labourd and Soule, and these provinces then had to be put down by force. In the year following, the *département* of Basses-Pyrénées (since 1971 Pyrénées-Atlantiques) was created. This area comprises the northern Basque Country and the Béarn, despite protests from both communities. It was at this time that the people of the northern Basque Country were forced to begin paying taxes to the French State and to do military service outside their own province. In 1794 the French authorities deported to the Landes several thousand inhabitants of the frontier districts of Labourd because they had refused to take up arms against their kinsmen in Navarra and Guipúzcoa. Most of them died in atrocious conditions.

After Napoleon's accession to power, Prefects were appointed who reinforced French centralism and brought in a system of compulsory education that was carried on exclusively in French, thus consigning the Basque language to the scrap-heap. The poverty and neglect of the northern Basque Country have continued over the last two hundred years and are the root-cause of the substantial emigration from these provinces to Bordeaux, Paris and especially America.

The first Carlist War 1833-39

Over the centuries the discontent of the southern Basques boiled over several times against foreign attempts to impose taxes or laws on them. For example, there were riots in Vizcaya in 1631, 1718 and 1766, the last two of which were known as Matxinadas, and another in 1804, called the Zamacolada, both in protest against compulsory military service.

At every stage of their history the Basques have taken advantage of the international political climate or the internal problems of the Spanish monarchy with a view to protecting their foral rights, which were a condition of their support for royalty but which the latter have always eroded. That is why, in 1794, at the outbreak of the War of the Convention in France, the first great separatist movement got

under way in the four provinces. This movement had the support of
Guipúzcoa, which allowed access over the border, and of the other
three provinces whose neutrality was guaranteed in exchange for a
recognition of their foral rights.

Under the Treaty of Basle in 1795, Spain won back the Basque
territories in exchange for ceding the eastern part of the island of
Santa Dominica, in the Caribbean, and promising not to take reprisals against Basques crossing the border into the three northern
provinces, a promise that was not kept. Indeed, they took very
seriously the lack of security in the northern provinces and used force
to accelerate the process of imposing constitutional unity, thus causing even more conflict.

However, being prevented from crossing the border was not all
that severe a restriction as long as the traditional rights of the
Basques were respected. This threat was renewed at the time of the
Francesada in 1813, and again in 1873, in 1876, and in 1893, at the
time of the Gamazada, to which we shall return later. So, three
hundred years after the conquest, there were still those in Navarra
who wished to cross the border whenever their 'rights, laws, usages
and customs' were not fully respected by the Spaniards.

But there is no doubt that the two Carlist Wars of the 19th
century provide the best example of the separatists' claims.The first
of these, between 1833 and 1839, was fought in all parts of Spain but
especially in the four provinces of the southern Basque Country,
where it took the form of an insurrection in defence of local traditions and foral rights. For seven years the Basques set about creating
their own State. It consisted of a flexible administrative system and
relied on a large measure of popular support which served as the
basis of a powerful army. The army's backbone, at least in the early
phase, consisted of a peasant militia drawn from all four provinces
that was known as 'the Basque-Navarrese army'.

The Carlist regime was set up in the areas liberated by its army,
but this territory did not include the four capitals of the southern
Basque Country; it took in only the Basque-speaking areas about
which we spoke in Chapter 2. The Carlist army patrolled the borders
of this region and demanded safe-conduct for its troops when crossing it. During the first war the only 'free zone' in the whole of the
Spanish State was therefore the one where the Basque language was
generally spoken, and this curious fact was to be repeated during the
second war. The rebel territory was coterminous with the Basque-
speaking areas, which leads us to think that, for the Basques of those
days, the Carlist Wars were essentially a means of protecting their
institutions, their laws and customs — their collective personality.

If it had been a simple dynastic or religious problem, the hold that Carlism had on the Basque Country would have been about the same, no more nor less, than that on other parts of the Spanish State. The Carlist regime established in the four provinces had its own king, its central Government with several Ministers, who were changed during the course of the war, its own judicial system, and its own administration. Even the Church was officially represented in the person of the Bishop of Leon, who also had his residence at the Carlist court.

The Spanish army suffered defeat after defeat at the hands of the Carlist general Zumalakarregi, the undisputed leader of the insurrection, and Spain was obliged to call in troops from England, France and Portugal. In 1839, a few years after the death of Zumalakarregi during the siege of Bilbao, the war ended with the Treaty of Bergera. This was a political solution upheld by the foreign powers, an agreement by which the Basques would lay down their arms and disperse their troops in exchange for the recognition of their foral rights. Despite this outcome, which was honourable but forced upon them, thousands of Basques would not accept the Treaty and went into exile, either into the northern parts of their country or else to America.

The Basques having given up their arms, the Spanish army then occupied the country, from which it had been absent for the previous seven years, but far from keeping their promise about maintaining foral rights, the nascent Spanish bourgeoisie began to pursue a policy of unification. Although by the terms of the Treaty of Abrazo the Spanish general had promised to respect foral rights, the law passed in that same year of 1839, after the Carlist defeat, stipulated with some subtlety that ' the foral rights of the Basque Provinces and of Navarra are confirmed without prejudice to constitutional unity'. In 1841 the Government, with the agreement of its allies in Navarra, promulgated the *Ley de Modificación de Fueros* (Law for the Modification of Foral Rights). After the implementation of this law the territory lost its status as a kingdom and became a province of Spain. Its border on the Ebro was replaced by the Pyrénées, a new system of taxation was introduced and compulsory military service brought in — the *quintas* — all of which caused serious disturbances in Navarra over the next eight years.

Despite the Government's attempts to bring about the same resolution in the rest of the southern Basque Country, the three other provinces managed to maintain the larger part of their foral structure, including their borders and exemption from military service, for another twenty-five years.

The second Carlist War 1872-76

In the years following this defeat, there was keen discontent throughout the southern Basque Country, which led a few decades later, in
1872 and up to 1876, to a new *'carlistada'* in the four provinces which
was financed by the *Diputaciones Provinciales.* For this reason they
earned the name *Diputaciones a Guerra.* These 'provincial' Governments once again set up a complex administrative system, introducing their own coinage and issuing their own postage stamps. The
main centres of this embryonic Basque State were in the towns of
Estella, Bergera and Durango. As for the town of Onate, it was the
seat of a University and the Supreme Court of Justice.

After the second Carlist defeat, almost all the foral privileges
enjoyed by the Basque provinces were abolished and compulsory
service was imposed there. It was precisely these measures which
obliterated the Basque Country after the loss of its foral rights and
which gave birth to the first Nationalist stirrings that were the direct
antecedents of the political and cultural movements of our own day.

Notable examples of the people's defence of Basque sovereignty
in the years after the Carlist Wars was the demonstration of 1893 in
the streets of Pamplona which brought out 80,000 people in protest
against an attempt by the Minister Gamazo to assimilate the taxation
system of Navarra into that of the rest of the Spanish State. This was
the first large mobilization of the Navarrese people of all ideologies
in defence of their foral rights. This event, which passed into history
as the *Gamazada,* succeeded in stopping, at least in part, the gradual
erosion of Navarrese rights. It is commemorated by the *Monumento
a los Fueros* in Pamplona, which was finished in 1903, and in the
names of many of the main squares in the villages of the Basque
Country. At the same time as these events in Navarra, and for much
the same reason, another huge demonstration took place in San
Sebastián against the presence of the Minister Sagasta. The song
sung on this occasion many times over, *'Gernikako Arbola',* was to
become the anthem associated ever after with the people's defence
of their foral rights. One year after the *Gamazada,* in 1894, during
another large demonstration held for the same purpose at Casteljón
in Navarra, there appeared for the first time, between the flags of
Navarra, an early version of the Basque flag. It was borne by the
founder of Basque Nationalism, Sabino Arana Goiri. The gathering
at Casteljón was therefore a symbol of continuity between Carlism
and Basque Nationalism.

After the second Carlist War, the collection of taxes, the running
of municipal administration, and other remnants of the foral sys-

tem, became the responsibility of the *Diputaciones*. This responsibility has continued to the present day in Álava and Navarra, and up to the end of the Civil War in 1939 in Guipúzcoa and Vizcaya. In these two provinces the *Conciertos Economicos* were reinstated in 1979, when the Statute of Autonomy was implemented in the so-called *'provincias vascongadas'*.

At the end of the 19th century and the beginning of the 20th, there was a vigorous movement in defence of Basque liberties and also, for the first time, of the Basque language, both of which were led by the Basque Nationalist Party. In 1932 the PNV organized the first *Aberri Eguna* in Bilbao, when an enormous crowd turned out to celebrate the national day. In 1902 *Euskaltzaleen Biltzarra* (*Unión de los Vasquistas*) was founded in the northern Basque Country. The political organization known as *Aintzina* was born in 1934. In 1918 the *Sociedad de Estudios Vascos* (Society of Basque Studies) was created and this body later became the Academy of the Basque Language, which covers the whole of the country.

The Civil War 1936-39

In June 1931, two months after the proclamation of the Spanish Republic, the Assembly of Basque Municipalities in the four southern provinces met at Estella and approved, by a large majority, what came to be known as the *Estatuto de Estella*. At the General Election held at the end of that year, candidates calling themselves 'Autonomy candidates', including Nationalists, Traditionalists and Independents, won a majority of the votes. But a series of intrigues manipulated from Madrid succeeded in breaking up this alliance and making the proposed unitary Statute unworkable.

On 18 July 1936, large sections of the Spanish Army, supported and financed by the upper class, rose against the Second Republic. This led to the implementation of the first Statute which had for three years been in abeyance. It had been ratified on 5 November 1933 and, what is more, by an overwhelming majority, 84% of the electorate, in favour. (By comparison, at the referendum for the Statute in place today, the one approved on 25 October 1979, the 'yes' vote amounted to only 53% of the electorate, on the same territory and in response to the same question.)

The 'Autonomous' Government, with José Antonio Aguirre at its head, upheld the legality of the Republic, as did the great majority of Basque citizens, some in order to promote the national cause, others the cause of the working class, and yet others quite simply in order to protect Republican liberties. It was for these reasons that

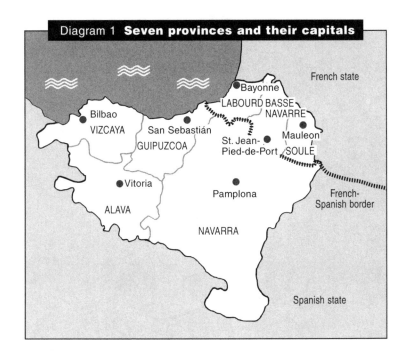

Diagram 1 Seven provinces and their capitals

French state

Bayonne
LABOURD BASSE
NAVARRE

Bilbao
VIZCAYA
San Sebastián
GUIPUZCOA
St. Jean-
Pied-de-Port
Mauleon
SOULE

Vitoria
ALAVA
Pamplona
French-
Spanish border

NAVARRA

Spanish state

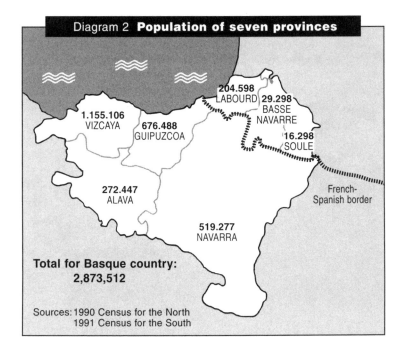

Diagram 2 Population of seven provinces

204.598
LABOURD 29.298
BASSE
NAVARRE

1.155.106
VIZCAYA
676.488
GUIPUZCOA
16.298
SOULE

272.447
ALAVA
French-
Spanish border

519.277
NAVARRA

**Total for Basque country:
2,873,512**

Sources: 1990 Census for the North
1991 Census for the South

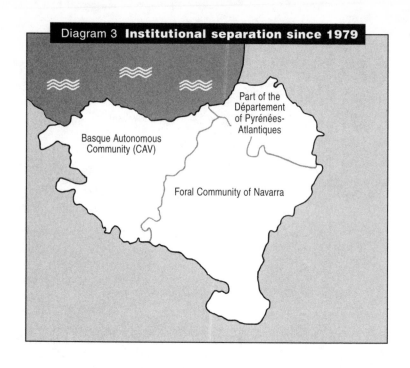

Diagram 3 **Institutional separation since 1979**

Part of the Département of Pyrénées-Atlantiques

Basque Autonomous Community (CAV)

Foral Community of Navarra

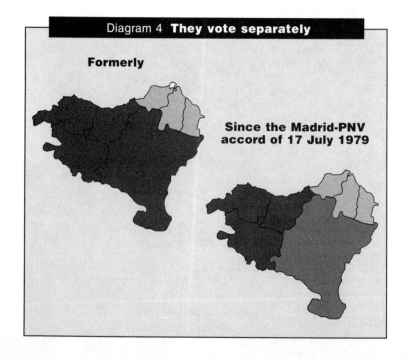

Diagram 4 **They vote separately**

Formerly

Since the Madrid-PNV accord of 17 July 1979

Diagram 3 The historical retreat of the Basque language

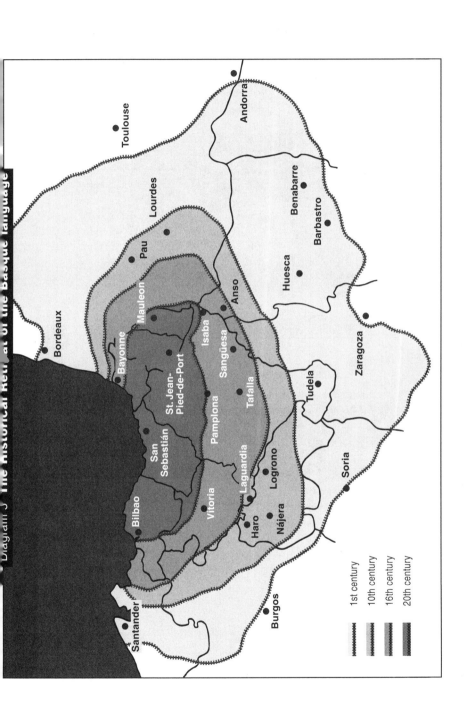

- Toulouse
- Andorra
- Benabarre
- Barbastro
- Lourdes
- Pau
- Huesca
- Mauleon
- Anso
- Bayonne
- Isaba
- Sangüesa
- Zaragoza
- Bordeaux
- St. Jean-Pied-de-Port
- Pamplona
- Tafalla
- Tudela
- San Sebastián
- Laguardia
- Logrono
- Soria
- Bilbao
- Vitoria
- Haro
- Nájera
- Burgos
- Santander

1st century
10th century
16th century
20th century

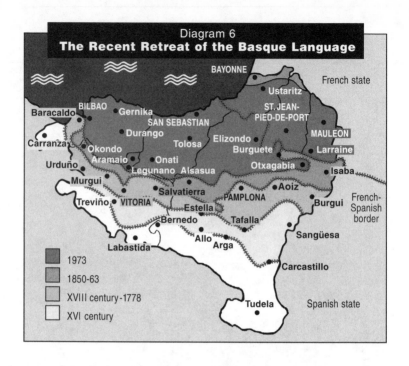

Diagram 6
The Recent Retreat of the Basque Language

French state

BAYONNE
Ustaritz
ST. JEAN-PIED-DE-PORT
MAULEON
Larraine
Baracaldo
BILBAO
Gernika
SAN SEBASTIAN
Durango
Tolosa
Elizondo
Burguete
Carranza
Okondo
Aramaio
Onati
Legunano Alsasua
Otxagabia
Isaba
Urduño
Murgui
Aoiz
French-Spanish border
Treviño
VITORIA
Salvatierra
PAMPLONA
Estella
Burgui
Bernedo
Tafalla
Allo
Sangüesa
Labastida
Arga
Carcastillo
Tudela
Spanish state

- 1973
- 1850-63
- XVIII century-1778
- XVI century

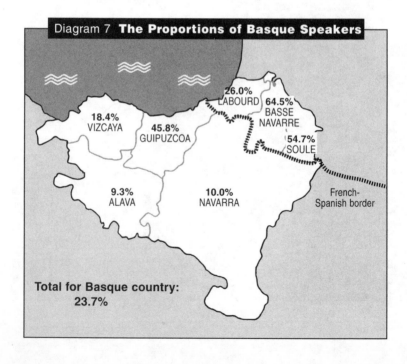

Diagram 7 The Proportions of Basque Speakers

26.0% LABOURD
64.5% BASSE NAVARRE
18.4% VIZCAYA
45.8% GUIPUZCOA
54.7% SOULE
9.3% ALAVA
10.0% NAVARRA
French-Spanish border

Total for Basque country: 23.7%

most of the Basque people joined the numerous battalions and
resistance groups opposed to the Spanish Army and its allies.
Navarra, on the other hand, was a stronghold of the insurgents.
Before setting out for the front in sister-provinces, however, the
insurgents had first to put down opposition in their own localities,
as the large number of deaths, more than 3,000 in all, bears witness
in an area which did not have a front of its own.

Finding it difficult to make any advance in Vizcaya, the insurgents
called in the Condor Legion of the German Army, which in the
Spring of 1937 bombed the villages of Durango and Guernica,
among others. This was the first aerial bombardment ever to be
unleashed on a non-combatant civilian population. Alarmed by
world-wide condemnation of the atrocity, the Spanish Army insisted
from the outset and for a long time afterwards, in the most hypocrit-
ical fashion, that it had been perpetrated by Republican forces.

As far as hostilities were concerned, the Civil War ended in the
Basque Country in June 1937 with the fall of Bilbao into the hands
of Franco's forces, which two years later were to dominate the
Spanish State. Political parties and trades unions were then banned,
the authority of Vizcaya and Guipúzcoa in fiscal matters (the *Conciertos Economicos*) was abolished, and a system of police interrogation and torture introduced which was to last to the present day.

The war in the Basque Country ended with 50,000 deaths, 10,000
prisoners, and 150,000 exiles. A number of these exiles continued to
fight Fascism in other parts of Europe during the Second World
War. As José María de Areilza, the mayor of Bilbao, put it in his
famous speech at the time: 'Vizcaya is once again a small part of
Spain as a result of military conquest alone.'

The Franco regime 1939-75

The demonstrations of Basque popular resistance against the new
regime were numerous but also very restricted. In 1947 all democratic groups in the Basque Country organized a week's general
strike which was followed by others in Vizcaya and Guipúzcoa, and
by yet more in 1951, 1953 and 1956. The group known as *Ekin*, the
embryo of what was to become *ETA*, was born in Bilbao in 1951.
Seven years later, towards the end of 1958, in Mondragón, the
foundation of co-operatives took place and the creation of Basque
schools in all the country's southern parts. In 1963 the group known
as *Enbata* was formed in the north and invited the first post-war
Aberri Eguna to be held at Itxasu in Labourd. At this gathering,
during which a cutting from the oak tree of Guernica was planted, a

Spanish Army police officer was recognized in the crowd. It was also the occasion when a manifesto was engraved on the stone of a monolith. The unity of the Basque people on both sides of the frontier was represented by a citizen of Hendaye and another from Bilbao who presided over the gathering.

The most famous episodes of Basque resistance to the Franco regime were the Burgos trials of December 1970 and, three years later, the assassination of the President of the Spanish Government, Admiral Carrero Blanco. It was in 1973, too, that the organization known as *Iparretarrak* was formed in the north.

During the fifteen years up to the death of Franco in November 1975, the struggle in the southern Basque Country for a change of national and social status was intense. It has included four general strikes of a political character, in which the entire population took part, despite very difficult conditions and the need for secrecy: in December 1970 against the Burgos trials; on 11 December 1974 in defence of civil liberties and for better economic conditions; on 11 June 1975 in protest against repression and the state of emergency; and in September 1975 against the execution of two *ETA* militants and three members of *FRAP* (the Spanish armed Communist group).

Six other general strikes of a political nature took place during the period usually called 'the transition', that is between the death of Franco and the first elections of June 1977: on 11 December 1975, a few days after the dictator's death, a general strike calling for an amnesty on 4 March 1976 in protest against the deaths while in police custody of several workers on strike in Vitoria; on 13 September 1976 in protest against the death at Fuentarrabia of a demonstrator struck down by police officers; on 27 September 1976 in support of a demand for an amnesty; on 10 March 1977 in protest against the death at Itxasu of two *ETA* members; and on 13 May 1977 in support of another demand for an amnesty.

The history of the Basque Country is one of continuous protest against imposed conditions, unremitting effort in defence of its identity and a relentless search for a means of democratizing its public life.

Chapter 6

DEMOCRACY AND TORTURE

Every year there are nearly a hundred reported cases of torture in the Basque Country. To this figure must be added those which go unreported, due to the victims' fear that they might have to relive this terrible experience. A single case will serve to illustrate the way in which the police habitually behave when interrogating suspects. The detainee in question was a Basque refugee who was handed over to the Spanish police by the French police without any extradition procedures or any judicial proceedings.

The case of Joxe Domingo Aizpurua

On 2 June 1994 Joxe Domingo Aizpurua, having served three years, was looking forward to finishing his four-year sentence in a French gaol. As the time came for him to be released from the prison of Fleury-Merogis, the French police re-arrested him while he was still inside the building — contrary to the law — and then handed him over to the Spanish Civil Guard at Irun. The following account, written by Aizpurua himself, relates the appalling torture which he suffered at their hands from the moment — it was 8.45 pm on a day he will remember for the rest of his life — when the police bundled him into a van in the border-town of Irun. The torture lasted several days, in both San Sebastián and Madrid, and he was in solitary confinement for a fortnight.

After appearing before the *Audiencia Nacional* without the services of a lawyer, he was eventually set free without caution and returned to his native village of Usurbil in Guipúzcoa, where he was given a warm welcome in a festive atmosphere by a huge crowd of sympathizers.

It might be thought that the French authorities are aware that to hand over a detainee to the Spanish State is quite a different matter from handing one over to Sweden or Italy, as far as the likelihood of torture is concerned. In any case, what happened to Aizpurua, and to many others before him, brings shame on a country of Republican traditions. What follows is the detainee's own testimony.

'I was put into an unmarked vehicle at the border, accompanied by three Civil Guards dressed as civilians. They made me lie on the back seat and, after covering my head with a pullover, they began beating me all over my body, on the head, the face, the stomach, the testicles, all the while hurling insults at me and threatening me.

'I was taken like this to the Civil Guard headquarters in San Sebastián, where they put a kind of blindfold or mask over my eyes which I had to wear throughout my detention, both in San Sebastián and Madrid. They took it off only for the visit of a doctor and for my appearance before an assistant solicitor.

'On my arrival at the police station in San Sebastián I was examined by a forensic attendant, who did not behave like a doctor at all. Immediately after the examination, with my eyes still blindfolded, I was subjected to a long interrogation and the most brutal torture which went on all night, without the slightest let-up, until about seven in the morning of Friday 3 June.

'The torture began as a kind of ritual. With my eyes still covered, I suddenly heard loud shouting, insults and threats. Two voices, more muffled than the rest, shouted into my ear and I could hear the sound of military footsteps all around me. They then put a sort of band around my wrists and began trying to shove a plastic bag over my head, a well-known way of quickly suffocating someone. Each time they put a bag over my head, one of the torturers would hold me gently by the wrists as if he were taking my pulse, and then he would give the others orders as to when precisely they should take off the bag. Three seconds later they put it back on again. And so on. They did this many times.

'They also used the plastic bag, electrodes and blows to all parts of my body. They would put the bag over my head between five and ten times and then apply the electrodes to my body, to my toes, my thighs, my legs, my testicles and my penis (particularly here), and to my mouth, my hands, and my chest. Afterwards they would offer me a glass of water and, as I took hold of it, they would apply the electrodes to my hands, which produced an even greater current. Whenever I screamed from the pain, they resumed their beating. They struck me on the face and chest with the palms of their hands in order not to leave any marks, then on the stomach and testicles with their fists. Then they delivered repeated blows to the head with a kind of book, which made me feel as if my head were swelling. Very often, before humiliating and insulting me, they took off my clothes, which made me panic completely because I thought they were going to put the electrodes on my bare flesh, but they never did that, they always applied them while I was dressed.

'All these methods which I have just listed were repeated without let-up and in regular sequence: sessions with the plastic bag, then the electrodes, and then the beatings. They stood around me and pushed me from one to the other as they hit me. From the outset they were threatening me and telling me that if I reported them to the judge or to *Egin* they would arrest my mother and put her in prison.

'Shortly before I was transferred from San Sebastián to Madrid, they put me in a cell in complete darkness, where they took off my blindfold, although I could see nothing. They made me stand upright against the wall, but having suffered so much during the previous night, I fainted — as I had done several times during the torture sessions. I remained lying on the floor of the cell, overcome by what is known as 'the discotheque effect': I could see little circles of shadow moving on the ceiling and wall, and I could hear only the cries of pain that I myself was making.

'Soon afterwards, once again, another group of torturers, I don't know how many, came into my cell and, putting something over my head, while all the time insulting and threatening me, they set about interrogating me all over again as I lay there on the floor. They then quickly got me to my feet in readiness for transferring me to Madrid.

'They took me blindfolded from the cell to the main gate of the prison and, once inside this gate, took off the mask. It was then I realized that I was inside the commissariat of the Civil Guard in the old quarter of San Sebastián. Seeing the light of day and that there was very little traffic in the streets outside, I thought it must have been about seven o'clock in the morning. Throughout that long night, they had given me nothing to eat or drink. But once again I was examined by that so-called doctor whom I mentioned earlier.

'They put me in a van belonging to the Civil Guard and drove me to Madrid. On leaving San Sebastián they put on some music and didn't turn it off until we reached our destination. The van was divided into several compartments, so that I couldn't see what was going on. In mine there was a speaker for playing music. And it was thus, in a foetal position, still shuddering from my beating and overcome by the long night of torture, that they took me to Madrid.

'On arriving at the headquarters of the Civil Guard in Madrid, they left me alone for a long time, some two hours in all, inside the van and in the stifling heat. They then pulled me out, covered my head with a pullover and dragged me to the dungeons, kicking and hitting me all the while. There, too, in the underground cell, I remained in darkness and when they brought me out for interrogation, they always did so with a blindfold over my eyes. I completely lost all sense of time. The interrogation sessions were numerous but I am unable to say exactly how many there were or when they took place. They didn't allow me to rest for long, bringing me out of the cell time and again to be interrogated. My interrogators continued to beat and threaten me without respite, but they didn't use the plastic bag or the electrodes.

'I was questioned several times by the forensic attendant, but I can't say how many times or how often. Whenever I asked him when he was going to come again, he wouldn't give me a definite answer, from which I guessed he was under the control of those who were torturing me. Whenever this man asked me whether I had eaten since his last visit, I could never remember. I had no control over my sense of time or any way of measuring it. They kept on threatening me that if I revealed to the doctor that I had been tortured they would torture me again. Because I was afraid of this, and because I thought there might be microphones hidden in the cell, I never mentioned the torture I had suffered to the doctor.

'It was the same when the assistant solicitor came to take my official statement. Once again they threatened to torture me if I should reveal to him what they had got out of me by torture. After I had made my statement, and up to the solicitor's next visit, the interrogations and torture began all over again. When I made my first statement, the lawyer was definitely an imposter, in fact a member of the Civil Guard. This seemed obvious to me, since at no time did the man give his name and also because, at the third or fourth session, he pretended to become ill and the statement was called off. The only times I was left without a blindfold, as I have said, were when I was making these statements and when the forensic attendant visited me.

'As for the behaviour of that man, I can say that whenever he examined me at the commissariat, he did not make me undress completely, but allowed me to remain in my underclothes. Strangely enough, five days after being sent to the prison of Carabanchel, the same doctor came to carry out one last medical check-up by order of the judge. This time he made me take off all my clothes and could therefore see the marks I had received on my stomach and testicles. As for the statements I made to the solicitor, once they were finished and he had left, the policemen threatened me by reminding me of the fate of Gurutze Yanci, whom the Civil Guard had tortured to death a little earlier.'

Torture today

Before the Socialist Party was returned to power in October 1982, it seemed clear that its leaders were opposed to torture as a means of police interrogation. In February 1981 there was the borderline case of a Basque militant who died after being tortured at the *Dirección General de Seguridad*, that is to say at the headquarters of the police force which has been famous since the time of Franco for the many terrible cases of torture carried out there. This building is situated in the middle of the *Puerta del Sol* in Madrid, just under the clock which keeps official time and near the central point of the road network.

The militant who was killed was a young man from Guipúzcoa, Joseba Arregi, who had been arrested on 4 February 1981. Nine days later, as a result of the torture he had suffered at the hands of several dozen police officers, he died within a few hours of being taken to the prison hospital of Carabanchel. This dreadful piece of news had such an effect on public opinion that on 16 February there was a general strike in all four provinces of the southern Basque Country and also a number of huge demonstrations.

On this occasion some of the most prominent leaders of the *PSOE* made statements denouncing torture. For example, José María Benegas, the Party's Executive Secretary, was reported in *El País* on 14 February 1981 as saying: 'The death of Joseba Arregi Izagirre, as a result of the torture he suffered during his detention, prompts us to reject and condemn torture in the strongest possible terms. This method of interrogation is a flagrant denial of the victim's most basic human rights and is intolerable in a democracy and in any State which is governed by law.'

Next day, this same newspaper carried the following statement by Enrique Mugica, who years later would become Minister of Justice in a Socialist Government: 'The pitiless murder of Joseba Arregi under torture, carried out by members of the *Cuerpo Superior de Policía*, must be severely punished. Certain ranks of the Security Corps share the responsibility for his death, for although they themselves did not actually commit the crime, they ensure that Fascist habits, customs and ideas persist among some of their members. It is only by rooting out these people that we shall be able to ensure basic freedoms and the spirit of democracy among those who are supposed to protect them.'

But when the Socialists came to power in the Spanish Government in October 1982, they seemed to abandon their opposition to 'Fascist habits'. A few days after their victory in Madrid, when there was betting in the Basque Country as to whether the Socialist Party would tolerate police torture or not, a well-known lawyer from San Sebastián had an opportunity of discussing the question with the province's recently elected Civil Governor. As the latter had expressed his disapproval of torture, the lawyer tried to find a way of helping to combat it, or at least of detecting it, and after making a number of proposals which were turned down, he made the Governor the following offer: 'Let us deal only with something that is not at all difficult. Simply this, whenever you hear of a detainee who is being tortured by the police in the cellars of the Civil Guard, you will go down into the cells and see the detainee for yourself, without any other obligation on your part.' After a slight hesitation the Governor declined, letting it be clearly understood that there were going to be further cases of torture and that he accepted them in advance.

In fact, that is what happened, as subsequent events have shown many times, despite all the official statements to the contrary. Barely a few months after the *PSOE* came to power in Madrid, the new Civil Governors of the southern Basque Country declared themselves against torture: 'As I take up this post,' said Julián San Cristobál, the new Governor of Vizcaya, in January 1983, 'I wish to give a cast-iron guarantee that from now on torture will no longer be countenanced.' At the same time, the new Governor of Navarra (who in 1994 was to be accused of corruption and flee abroad) gave the same assurance: 'Torture has no place in our constitutional set-up and we shall weed it out.'

In this very province, however, the terrible news then broke that a young detainee from Pamplona, Mertxe Gonzalez, had been subjected to torture, which she was to describe as follows: 'The worst of it was when they took off my clothes. They squeezed by breasts very hard, put a broom-handle into my vagina, made me change my tampon while they looked on, and then put it into my mouth. After they had finished hitting me, they began pawing me and then they took me back to my cell. Later on, they threatened to take me into the mountains and finish me off.' This news shook public opinion to such an extent that the Municipal Council of Pamplona, consisting mainly of the *PSOE*, the Conservative *UPN*, and *Herri Batasuna* (the Conservative *PP* abstaining), categorically condemned 'the torture that exists within the Spanish State'. The Council also took the side of Mertxe Gonzalez, to whom it referred as 'a person who has been tortured, raped, and attacked with a quite exceptional degree of sadism.' As for the Governor of Navarra, the self-same Roldán who had made such unequivocal statements against torture when he first took up his post, not only did he refuse to support the Municipal Council in its condemnation, but told the prosecution that it had agreed with it, 'lest he be thought to have committed a criminal offence'.

Condemnation of police torture was widespread at this time, at least in theory. The Councillor of the Interior in the Government of Vitoria, Luis Mariá Retolaza, said on 11 March 1982: 'The Basque Government is aware that torture goes on in the police stations, but we have no power whatsoever for dealing with it.'

Another case of torture which caused a huge outcry was that of Mikel Zabalza, also from Navarra, who was arrested by the Civil Guard in November 1985. His corpse, with handcuffs still on its wrists, was found twenty days later, floating in the waters of the river Bidasoa. The repercussions of this shocking crime were so strong that the general strike called for 18 December won the unanimous support of all four provinces. That the strike was called before the authorities gave their account of the crime is clear proof of the total distrust felt by the Basques of the official versions of such events. When it became known that other young people arrested at the same time as Zabalza had also been horribly tortured, their worst suspicions were confirmed.

Another case concerns two Basques who had been deported to Ecuador. In January 1986 Spanish police officers who had gone to Ecuador, removed the prisoners from the custody of the authorities there, took them to a lonely spot and inflicted savage torture on them during interrogation, including long sessions of strangulation and the use of electrodes. Perhaps the most widely known case is that of Andoni Murelaga from Vizcaya who was arrested and tortured in April 1990 by the *Ertzaintza* (the Autonomous Police Force of the *CAV*). On account of its being the first case of torture laid at the door of this new force, which had been created under the Constitution and Statute of Autonomy out of the corps which had existed in Franco's time, the case shocked public opinion and caused the Basques greater grief than is usual on these occasions. The detention of the young man from Vizcaya was warmly welcomed by the Spanish Minister of the Interior and, a few days later, the two heads of the Interior Ministries in Madrid and Vitoria came to an agreement on the use of the *Ertzaintza.* Andoni Murelaga appeared before the judge with his arms badly bruised and his jaw swollen. His testicles were also said to be swollen and he had difficulty in passing urine, because the police officers had been assaulting him. But those who had tortured this young man were acquitted for lack of evidence.

In September 1993 two Basque detainees died under torture while in police custody. These were Gurutze Yanci, who has already been mentioned, killed by the Civil Guard in Madrid, and Xabier

Kalparsoro, a young man who lost his life in a police station in Vizcaya.

We draw attention to these particular cases because of the unusual impact they had on public opinion at the time. In fact, they do not give a full picture of the use of torture in the Basque Country, which now runs into hundreds of incidents. Most attract no special attention because they take place almost every day.

Torture usually consists of beatings, particularly about the head and neck, physical exhaustion, asphyxiation by putting the victim's head in a plastic bag, immersion in water to the point of drowning, application of electrodes to all parts of the body but especially the sexual organs, sexual aggression of both a physical and psychological kind, threats, mock-executions, and the forcing of prisoners to watch or listen to torture being inflicted upon others. This is how, during a press conference, a young man who had undergone this treatment described it to us: 'I had never before had any experience of electrodes. It's as if your whole body is being torn apart, it makes you want to vomit, it tugs at your entrails. It's like a red-hot iron burning inside you, like a scalpel ripping your flesh to shreds.'

In 1993 a total of 84 detainees stated before a judge that they had been tortured in police stations. In 1992 there had been 118 recorded cases and 64 in 1991. Between 1982, the year of the *PSOE*'s electoral victory, and 1990, a total of 484 cases were reported.

Such is the terror on the part of a detainee after an experience such as this that he very often prefers not to admit that he has been tortured, or does not dare to do so, for fear that he will be tortured again. The real number of torture cases is always, for this reason, higher than the official estimate.

Whenever questions about the use of torture were put to Felipe González, or to the Ministers of the Interior who succeeded him, or to any other of the Madrid authorities, they always avoided giving a direct answer, saying: ' There is no torture. What happens is that members of *ETA* who have been detained have orders to systematically complain that they have been tortured.' In fact, the authorities of all kinds (those belonging to the Spanish State and the French) know perfectly well that the use of torture is something that goes on all the time in police stations and the smaller Spanish barracks. Basque public opinion is also aware of it, at first-hand. We must recognize, on the other hand, that Spanish public opinion has no knowledge of torture. Most Spaniards would not even dare to think about these appalling matters and the fact that torture is almost a daily occurrence.

The claim that Basque militants are under orders to make up

reports of torture and that, as a consequence, the number of cases reported is higher than the actual number, has no foundation whatsoever. In fact, the opposite is true. The police torturers are in the habit of letting detainees go with the warning that they should tell no one about what has happened if they want to avoid being tortured again. But the most decisive way of keeping the detainee quiet is not this particular warning; what ensures his silence is the indescribable horror of having to live in a body which has been subjected to such interrogation.

Whenever they find they have no way out of admitting an obvious case of torture, and of avoiding the scandal that goes with it, the authorities usually say that it is an isolated case, that torture does not exist and that it is the militants who make a point of complaining about it. The reality, unfortunately, is precisely the opposite. Torture is systematic: 'they torture us as a matter of routine', one detainee has written. There may very well be isolated cases of alleged torture which will not stand up to scrutiny, but most of those reported correspond to the sad reality of the situation.

For the police it is a matter not only of torturing, but of torturing without leaving any marks. This is the difficult part of their job. It is easy to cause a lot of pain, especially when there is no risk of interruption during the session and the cries of the victim cannot be heard. What is more difficult is to torture someone without leaving any visible signs on the body, because this limits the number of times a person can be assaulted and the ways in which the interrogation can be carried out. It would make no sense if torture were to be verifiable, because it would be immediately rejected as a means of interrogating the prisoner. Modern society would not tolerate it.

For the police, it is as important to conceal the method of torture as it is to terrorise a prisoner during interrogation. Whenever they are interviewed and make statements, the names of the torturers are not given and they take care to wear hoods so as not to be recognized, or else a hood is put over the head of the detainee. As the authorities know full well, torture makes sense only when it is impossible to prove.

For this reason the protection of the torturer is very important. The man who has been assigned this ignoble and degrading task must be certain that his boss will not send him to prison just because he has done his duty. The complicity of politicians and the passivity of the *Audiencia Nacional* who try detainees accused of belonging to *ETA*, and before whom some appear obviously broken by torture, or who have to be taken to hospital immediately, are also essential.

In the police force, which is a leftover from the days of Franco, contacts are kept up with citizens who are still ready to obey an authoritarian regime. Blows and insults are the common stock-in-trade of ordinary policemen. On the other hand, what is usually called torture — for example, the use of electrodes on the detainee's body — is not a practice that all policemen can go in for; it is reserved in each force for a small élite of officers. This provides another guarantee, not only of specialization (such as skill in causing pain while avoiding any excess that might be reported) but also of the greatest discretion in carrying out this task. The ordinary policemen confine themselves to co-operating by remaining silent, even denying that torture is used, but they do not go in for it themselves.

Torture was introduced as a common practice of the Spanish police following Franco's insurgence against the legitimate Republic on 18 July 1936. It has been used to varying degrees ever since but consistently against Basque militants. Police torture under Franco became so notorious that the Spanish Constitution includes an article which expressly prohibits it; there is no such clause in the Constitution of any other European State. Article 25 of the Spanish Constitution stipulates: 'Everyone has a right to life and to moral and physical well-being, without being subjected in any way to torture or to any treatment that is inhuman or degrading.' But it is evident that this clause has not been put into practice.

Modern society declares itself to be opposed to torture and the overwhelming majority of citizens in every State deplore its practice. This was not the case in times gone by, for torture used to be publicly acknowledged, in theory and practice. But nowadays it is no longer a subject for debate. Today there are people who are in favour of the death penalty and others who are against it, just as there exist people who are for or against euthanasia or the rights of homosexual couples. These matters are topics for public discussion, on which there are differences of opinion. Torture does not belong to this category of polemical topics because there is no public discussion of it.

The suppression of this shameful method of police interrogation demands, in the first place, that the public become aware of it. The alcoholic is able to cure himself only when he begins to recognize publicly that he suffers from alcoholism. In the same way, torture will not disappear as long as its existence is kept in the shadows. It is for this reason that the victim's voice must be directly heard by the public. The Spanish authorities have never given up this method of police interrogation. Nor are they likely to do so before reaching a democratic solution to the Basque problem. They endeavour to cover up torture, to deny its existence, in particular by making sure that the voice of the tortured is not heard. At the same time they try to use torture in a selective way, limiting it to cases where they are most likely to achieve results.

The frequent use of torture was so widespread under Franco that, sixty years on, it is no exaggeration to say that everyone in the southern Basque Country knows someone in their family, in their neighbourhood, or among their friends, who has been a victim of torture. The social impact of torture, as a collective phenomenon, should not be under-estimated; it can be compared, in its psychological consequences, to the social impact of a civil war. In this lies the significance of the saying *'que se vayan'* ('let them leave'), used in connection with the Spanish police, which became so common during the years of transition. The denial of torture is a question that should be laid at the door of the State and one which the Spanish authorities have to answer, but it is they who go to extreme lengths to protect the impunity of the torturers.

Nevertheless, the fact that the public is aware of this practice — at least the Basque public, whereas Spaniards have only a vague idea of what is going on — deprives the Government of all moral authority. The Government is thus able to carry out repression despite the handicap of the public's awareness of the practice. On the other hand, under these conditions, it becomes more difficult for the Government to carry out its principal function, that of governing, and ensuring the moral conduct of society. The existence of torture is a moral dilemma but for the Spanish authorities it is more than that. For them, torture is an inescapable necessity, for as long as they refuse to recognize the Basques' right to sovereignty. Torture is an effective part of interrogation because it gets results. As the police themselves say, albeit in cruder terms, 'If we don't beat you up, you won't give us any names.'

The Basque movement — in its public demonstrations but also, in particular, by its armed struggle — is very difficult to combat without the use of torture. The Spanish authorities do not torture people out of perversity but because they are not democratically accountable, and so they are able to suppress the Basques more effectively. It is not difficult to defeat an armed group without having recourse to police methods so odious as torture. The essential thing is to isolate the group from the population, so that it is deprived of a political base among the people. When it can rely on such bases, the group flourishes and grows in strength. Then torture is necessary for the obtaining of names.

The prevailing moral philosophy in Europe in the 20th century condemns torture whatever the circumstances might be. But if the

Government tries to crush political armed opposition by force, without giving it a means of arriving at a political solution, if it attempts to impose its own viewpoint, it will find itself having to use torture. It will be a condition of the politics of repression that the Government imposes upon itself. And so, anti-democratic behaviour — in this case, the denial of Basque self-determination — leads to further anti-democratic behaviour on its part: the use of torture.

International bodies

The involvement of a number of international bodies in the question of torture has not been sufficient to root it out, for as we have said, if there is no democratization of the way in which the Spanish Government behaves towards the Basques, torture will continue as before. All the same, this involvement is as valuable as public denunciation of a reality which would otherwise remain hidden from the eyes of other European countries. For the Basques, the existence of torture does not need to be demonstrated because they have direct experience of it through those close to them in whom they have every confidence. The reports of Amnesty International and other organizations are not absolutely necessary as far as they are concerned. What is more, the Basques take the view that these reports always gather too small a number of cases. But as the present book is intended for readers in other parts of Europe, who may be inclined to doubt the description of torture when it is too subjective and at second hand, or when torture takes place in foreign parts, it is relevant to quote from international reports on torture by the Spanish authorities.

The United Nations Commission on Human Rights, in its special report for the years 1992 and 1993, condemned eight specific cases of torture inflicted on detainees and prisoners held in Spanish gaols, in which many police officers and civil servants were implicated but not brought to trial. We have chosen to reproduce here, from among the eight cases described in the report, the account given by Kepa Urra, who was arrested in January 1992, as follows.

'As soon as I was arrested, they took me into the mountains and, on the way, they began squeezing my testicles and hitting me all over my body. They threatened me all the while. Once we were in the mountains, they took off my underpants, my tee-shirt, my trainers and my watch, before starting a sort of macabre ritual: blows to my ears, then all over my body, but especially about the head and to my testicles.

'They put the barrel of a revolver to my head, they took off the safety-catch and then squeezed the trigger. I received blows to all parts of my body from a rubber truncheon, and then karate chops to my neck and stomach . . They then started throttling me, using the thumb and the index-finger, until I was nearly strangled. In the barracks of the Civil Guard in Bilbao, the same thing happened again: first I was beaten and then they put a plastic bag over my head, until they got fed up with torturing me. When they started with the bag they made me put on a pair of overalls.

'In the cell, they left me lying on the floor. Every now and then they would come in and kick me in the kidneys. Once, a pair of them took me to see someone they said was a doctor. This man took my pulse and told me that I was suffering from arythmia.

'In the hospital at Basurto I was better, but there was torture there, too. They came into my room twice and I had to call for help, as a nurse later confirmed.'

Urra, the report concluded, was admitted to hospital in a state of shock, according to the emergency unit. The doctors found numerous lesions, inflammation and haematomas of a reddish-purple colour, as well as wounds to the right eyelid, a blackish haematoma on the abdomen and two lesions on the neck.

The report was presented by the British Labour politician Nigel Rodley, who had been commissioned by the United Nations to look into the question of torture in Spain. After finishing his work, he tried to get out of the Spanish Government its version of events. The Government replied on 13 December 1993, claiming that detainees always have access to legal and medical assistance while in custody and that 'if *ETA* terrorists are in the habit of complaining about torture, it is only a ploy to undermine the reputation of the security forces'.

As for the specific case of Urra, the Government attributed the frightful state of the detainee on being admitted to the hospital in Basurto to injuries he had received during his detention, 'with which he would not comply'.

The UN report certified that the solitary confinement into which detainees are put, sometimes for as long as five days at a time, often goes with the practice of torture, as several other experts have confirmed. The report also deplored the fact that the policemen accused of torturing suspects had not been removed from service, that some had even been absolved, and that whenever there are inquiries into cases of torture, the proceedings usually last years.

The Accord 'against torture and other cruel, inhuman or degrading treatment' was published in New York on 10 December 1984 and the Spanish State ratified it on 19 October 1987. The Committee against Torture, which is made up of ten experts from among the signatories, works to this Agreement.

An earlier report by Peter Kooijmans gathered evidence of torture from some twenty Basques arrested in January and February 1992. The most common methods used against these detainees were the application of electrodes, the plastic bag and sexual harassment, particularly of women. The European Parliament also commissioned its own reports in the interests of protecting the citizens of its member States from torture. In 1993 it presented the De Gucht Report, in which several cases of torture by the Spanish police were described. In 1994 the same body published the Newman Report, which was prepared by the British expert Edward Newman. According to this report, 'the only way of guaranteeing the non-existence of torture is to consider it a serious offence, and not to allow its perpetrators to enjoy impunity'.

It added: 'The Committee against Torture, which was set up under the aegis of the UN Convention, receives reports from time to time from the States which are signatories. In April 1993 the Committee expressed its concern about the increase in the number of torture cases and the delay in dealing with them. It was of the view that Spain should adopt measures guaranteeing the implementation of the Convention.' It also noted that 'States such as Spain which have signed the Convention are obliged to examine cases of torture and to take legal action against those responsible. Very often, however, the inquiries take too long a time and the police officers found guilty are not systematically removed from service.' The Spanish State ratified the European Convention for the Prevention of Torture and Inhuman and Degrading Treatment on 2 May in Strasbourg.

Apart from the UN Committee against Torture and the European Parliament, the body which has the longest experience and shown the greatest perseverance in condemning the torture practised by the Spanish police is doubtless Amnesty International. To read the reports of this body over the last ten years or so is an overwhelming experience. Every year, without exception, Amnesty International condemns time and time again specific cases of torture inflicted by the Spanish police, usually against Basque militants, and not a year goes by without its deploring the lack of preventative measures and legal reform, as well as the hypocrisy of the official Spanish responses and the failure to punish those who carry out torture.

The clear nature of the evidence in these reports and the veracity of this body's inquiries and conclusions are unimpeachable. They also take into account various approaches made by Amnesty International to the Spanish Government, the French Government, the

UN and other bodies, in attempts to deal with this serious problem. But in the end they conclude by deploring the lack of interest on the part of Governments, putting it on record that the Spanish police in particular, having an attitude that is completely different from other police forces in Europe, persist in the use of torture against those whom they interrogate.

Chapter 7

REPRESSION BY MADRID AND PARIS

The intense but selective repression which goes on throughout the Basque Country is characteristic of the way the Spanish State is structured. It includes the illegal activity of torturing detainees, the policy of 'shoot to kill', the beating of prisoners, and various other para-police methods. All this goes on with the French State's connivance, whether discreet or brazen, depending on the climate of the day. If there were no repression of this kind, France and Spain would not be able to go on denying the Basque people's right to exist, nor would they be able to contain the dispute.

Shoot to kill

The Amnesty International report for the year 1993 ended on a note which links the question of torture with another method used by the Spanish police: it refers to 'the suspected murders carried out by the security forces in controversial circumstances or in circumstances that have not been properly investigated'. The suspected murders to which the report refers are the deaths of militants before they are apprehended. There have been many cases in which the police have killed militants when they should have confined themselves to arresting them without running any other risk. This is a practice commonly known as *'tirar a matar'* (shoot to kill) or *'fusilamientos encubiertos'* ('covert shootings'), which is just as illegal as torture but which nevertheless is quite common; it never leads to any official action on the part of the authorities. It is illegal but tolerated by those responsible for it.

The cases for which we have been able to gather details in recent years are as follows:

16.2.84 Barakaldo	Iñaki Ojeda
22.3.84 Pasaia	Pedro Mari Isart
22.3.84 Pasaia	Rafael Delas

22.3.84 Pasaia	Dionisio Aizpuru
22.3.84 Pasaia	José Mari Izura
15.6.84 Hernani	Juan Luis Lekuona
15.6.84 Hernani	Agustín Arregi
7.8.84 Oiartzun	Eduardo Irizar
13.8.84 Lasarte	Pablo Gude
15.1.86 San Sebastián	Alejandro Auzmendi
15.1.86 San Sebastián	Bakartxo Arzelus
15.1.86 San Sebastián	Luis Mari Zabaleta
23.7.87 Pasaia	Luzia Urigoitia
23.9.88 San Sebastián	Mikel Kastresana
16.9.89 Irun	Manu Urionabarrenetxea
16.9.89 Irun	Juan Oiarbide
25.6.90 Lumbier	Susana Arregi
25.6.90 Lumbier	Jon Lizarralde
18.9.90 Pamplona	Mikel Castillo
30.5.91 Llica d'Amunt	Joan Carles Monteagudo
30.5.91 Llica d'Amunt	Jon Félix Erezuma
17.8.91 San Sebastián	Jokin Leunda
17.8.91 San Sebastián	Iñaki Ormaetxea
17.8.91 San Sebastián	Patxi Itziar
29.8.91 Bilbao	Juan Mari Ormazabal

This is not a list of all Basque militants killed by the police (the total is nearly 150 since the emergence of *ETA*); it includes only the names of those killed by police without there being any armed confrontation, that is to say those who should only have been arrested.

More beatings

There are at any one time about 500 political prisoners in Spanish gaols and 50 in French. The conditions under which they are held are similar to those of prisoners held under the civil law, although there are important differences.

The International Prisons Commission is a non-governmental body with its offices in the town of Lyon. Its function is to draw attention to prisoners' living conditions and to work for this marginalized section of society. It also strives to improve the conditions under which prisoners are held. In May 1994, in Paris, this body published its report for the previous year. The following paragraphs will serve as a summary.

The prisons run by the French State are on the whole more up-to-date than those in Spain, although they are over-crowded, like the one at Bayonne where there are twice as many prisoners as the number for which it was built. As a general rule, the cost of food in the canteens is high, the hygiene in the older prisons poor, and medical attention deficient. But the worst thing about them seems to be the way in which prisoners are treated, not only insofar as they are sometimes abused but in that there is no rationale for the hard and rigid living conditions which prevail.

The Spanish gaols are in an even worse condition. The preliminary summary of the report carried out by the Commission, with which two prisoners' support groups co-operated, namely *Salhaketa* and *Senideak,* describe these prisons as over-crowded, in dilapidated buildings, where brutal acts and degrading customs are routine. Cases of torture have been reported in these gaols. The Basque detainees, about 500 in all, have been subjected to a very harsh regime since the policy of dispersing them was introduced in 1987.

The maltreatment, harassment and humiliation go on all the time. In 1993 there were many beatings, threats and constant searches of the cells and personal effects, during which the prisoners' things were broken or stolen. Very often during these searches, prisoners are made to undress and stand motionless in the middle of their cells. If they refuse, the warders remove their clothes by force. These scenes are sometimes accompanied by aggression on the part of the warders and end in solitary confinement for the prisoners. The roll-call also creates problems. It sometimes happens that warders waken the detainees in the middle of the night, using very intimidatory methods. They bang on cell doors, shouting loudly, bring bright lights into the cells and make the prisoners get out of bed, and when they have finished, they leave the lights on all night.

The physical condition of some of these prisons is atrocious: the equipment is worn out, inadequate and in a poor state of repair. The packing together of prisoners makes for the spread of disease. The heating system often breaks down. The exercise yards are usually too cramped. It appears that about twenty large gaols need to be built so that the older, dilapidated ones can be closed down.

The food is inadequate and of poor quality. It is too fatty and lacks fruit and green vegetables. Some prisons have no dining halls; in those that do, they often have to make do as common rooms. Prisoners find it very difficult to buy provisions and, if they can, food is very expensive. The standard of hygiene is very low. Filth and squalor are everywhere, leading to illness and contamination. If there are no rats, there are fleas, lice, and other kinds of insects and parasites. The showers have no privacy and often lack hot water. From a hygienic point of view, the standards of Spanish gaols belong to the Third World, to such an extent that living conditions are often harder to bear than incarceration itself. It is very difficult to combat disease in these gaols because three-quarters of the inmates are drug-addicts and half are HIV-positive. The clinics are badly equipped and there is a shortage of doctors and nurses. Medical inspections from outside are often forbidden, as the majority of Basque prisoners have come to learn since the policy of dispersing them was introduced.

It is no coincidence that nine Basque prisoners have already died in prison, often because of an error in diagnosis or in the medical treatment they have been given. To quote a few recent examples: in 1986 the prisoner Joséba Asensio, nearing the end of his sentence, was found dead in his cell as the result of tuberculosis which had not been diagnosed by the doctors. In the year following, Josu Retolaza died from a cancer which had been diagnosed as a simple verruca. In 1988 Juan Carlos Alberdi died of a heart-attack in his cell. Two years later, Mikel Zalakain died from a myocardial infarction, after suffering several attacks that had not been properly treated.

The report of the International Prisons Commission rightly noted: 'We must learn not to speak of natural deaths in prison. Death from natural causes usually happens towards the end of a man's life and not at the age of thirty, even if he is in detention.' Neither death from avoidable or poorly treated diseases, nor suicide, nor any other premature death in prison can be considered as death from natural causes.

Since the Spanish Ministry of Justice brought in a policy of dispersing prisoners to various parts of the Spanish State, whenever Basque detainees fall ill, their condition is aggravated by the fact that they are hundreds of kilometres away from their homes, so that their relatives are unable to visit them easily. Hospital visits take place under such difficult circumstances imposed by the police that a number of prisoners have preferred not to be visited by their families.

As for the recreation facilities inside the gaols, few of any kind are provided and it sometimes happens that Basque prisoners are denied access to them. Another treatment reserved for Basques is the refusal of parole when the date arrives. Family visits are rare and of short duration. They are supervised by warders and it is forbidden to speak Basque. Correspondence is allowed only infrequently and letters are confiscated if they are written in Basque; post is sometimes delayed by as much as a year.

The policy of dispersion that was brought in a few years ago was based on the notion that, separated from one another, *ETA* members would be isolated and readier to see the error of their ways.In implementing this policy the Government has violated the general principle, upheld in prison systems in other parts of the world, that prisoners must be held in gaols as close as possible to their homes, so that their family links can be maintained. The prisoner is also separated from his comrades, which results under such harsh conditions in psychological disorders. He also encounters incredible obstruction when trying to find opportunities for study.

In recent years an extra punishment for Basques has been the continual transfer of prisoners from gaol to gaol. This instability prevents them from undertaking any task or making any kind of plan. Very often a prisoner's family is not informed of his transfer and, when they arrive at the prison to visit him, they are told that he has been moved, but they are not informed as to why he has been transferred or where he has been taken. In some instances they are only told a few days afterwards. The distance between the prisoner and his family means that visits are very expensive and in some cases the cost is prohibitive. When to this are added the risks that have to be run, the obstacles to be overcome, whether on account of old age or some other personal factor, this policy of dispersion amounts to a heavy punishment for prisoners' families and friends. The transfer of Basque prisoners is one of the forms of pressure constantly applied to this group. In 1993 there were nearly 500 such transfers, usually in very harsh conditions: prisoners were handcuffed and put into vans and transported for particularly long distances. Another feature of these transfers is the frequent loss of private effects, such as books and other materials necessary for study, so that prisoners are often prevented from pursuing their studies while in gaol. However, the most serious injustice of the policy is doubtless the fact that during these transfers the Civil Guards, who are used for this work, beat up the prisoners while in transit. In 1993 there were no fewer than a hundred instances of this kind of terrifying aggression.

The beating of prisoners during detention takes place in two ways: it is sometimes inflicted on a group of prisoners, usually because of some protest or other, or else only one prisoner is involved; the latter has become more common now that prisoners are in transit all over Spain, but it also occurs while prisoners are being taken to court or even inside the prison itself. Individual beatings are almost always without reason and have no legitimate excuse. The police officers rain blows on the prisoner quite simply in order to express their hatred of him or knowing they can get away with it. The first beating of a group of prisoners after the *PSOE* came to power took place in the prison of Alcalá Meco in December 1982, after the inmates had protested to the Governor about the lack of heating in the cold conditions of the Castilian plain. The Governor, at the time under orders from a Socialist Minister, called in the National Police who went into the gaol and violently attacked the prisoners. The abuse of prisoners, besides being prohibited by law, is tantamount — according to the morality of the 20th century — to intolerable cruelty and cowardice. However, after the coming to power of the *PSOE*, it became common practice in Spain. It was resumed on a large scale when the talks in Algiers between the Spanish Government and *ETA* ended in 1989. It was then also that the policy of dispersion was reinforced. Since then, the yearbooks published by *Egin* have carried details of the long and terrifying suffering of prisoners both inside gaols and in transit. In 1992 there were 41 reported beatings and in 1993 the number went up to 93. The UN Commission on Human Rights, in its reports for 1992 and 1993, drew particular attention among the eight cases of maltreatment of Basque prisoners, to the brutal beating inflicted on Koldo Arrese in September 1992 by warders in the prison of Daroca in Zaragoza.

The way in which Basque prisoners are treated is so deplorable and so primitive that, together with police torture, it brings lasting shame on the Spanish State. Not all the pages in this book and our richest vocabulary would be enough to describe the many sacrifices and humiliations to which prisoners and their families have been subjected. The prisoners' struggle against their unjust living conditions has been a long and hard one, including hunger-strikes and '*chapeos*' (when prisoners refuse to leave their cells). Some of these tactics have been successful. But the punishment for any kind of protest is always out of all proportion and prolonged solitary confinement, one of the most common punishments, is usually accompanied by serious psychological risk to the prisoner.

The way in which prisoners are officially treated is in vivid contrast to how they are greeted on their release in their own villages or streets: a large number of their neighbours celebrate their release with Basque dancing, enormous feasts and other forms of merry-making. These celebrations are in themselves a sign that Basque prisoners are popular and fully integrated into local society.

Extraditions, deportations and expulsions

Extradition implies a judicial decision after examination of the application and all other circumstances. The French tradition which took shape during the Franco years was to refuse to grant extradition in the case of political refugees on account of the existence of police torture in the Spanish State. This tradition was maintained during the mandate of the *UCD*, the party of the Spanish Right which succeeded the Franco regime and, even during the first two years of the Socialist mandate. A short while after the electoral victory of the

French Left, the annual conference of the French Socialist Party, held at Metz in 1979, passed the following motion: 'Taking into account the serious consequences which they could suffer, we demand the re-establishment of the law of refuge for those Basques seeking political asylum in France and we will not accept that any person living in our midst is extradited for political reasons.'

During the short lapse of time between the French Socialist victory on 10 May 1981 and the Spanish Socialist victory on 10 October 1982, French leaders openly upheld the traditional position. On 9 July 1981, Robert Badinter, the French Minister of Justice, gave an assurance with regard to the Basques: 'France will always be a land of refuge for political refugees.' The old Republican traditions of France were still being upheld at this time. The French Minister of the Interior, Gaston Defferre, was even more explicit. When *Le Nouvel Observateur* asked him, in its edition of 18 July 1981, whether there was going to be any extradition of Basques, he replied: 'That is not possible, no. Perhaps because I myself know what it is to lead a clandestine life, I am firmly convinced that to allow extradition would be contrary to French tradition, especially when it is a question, as it is at present, of a political struggle.'

The first extradition of Basque refugees was granted by the French State towards the end of September 1984, after strong pressure had been brought to bear by the Spanish Socialist Government on the French Government, which was also Socialist. This extradition led to a general strike on the 26th of the same month which had general support throughout the Basque Country. Since then the number of Basques extradited has risen to 30, 26 of whom were delivered up by the French State and the rest by others. This figure includes only extraditions in the strict sense, that it to say those who were handed over to Spanish courts by means of judicial procedures; many more were delivered up by other means.

There is a fallacy at the heart of the about-turn by the French authorities, who first refused to extradite and then decided to do so. It is true that the Spanish regime, after Franco's death, appeared to have changed into a democratic State, it may be true that the Spanish regime is similar enough to other European democracies, but this should also have meant the suppression of police torture. The Spanish Constitution explicitly prohibits torture, as we have already seen.

For most Europeans it was difficult to argue with the recognition of the Spanish State as a democracy under the mandate of the *UCD*, despite the fact that a number of its members had served the Franco regime. It became even more difficult when in 1982 the Socialist Party was elected to Government, a party which had lost the Civil

War and was considered to be on the Left of the political spectrum. The rejection of extradition was a routine that belonged to the past and it had no raison d'être in the new political context, or so it was said.

That is where the fallacy lies. It is true that democratic liberties and the prohibition of torture by the Constitution encouraged the presumption that it had indeed been abolished, but this did not amount to proof, as the facts have subsequently shown. The Spanish State has even signed international agreements aimed at doing away with torture. But it has not got rid of torture, nor even limited its use. The French State, by sleight of hand, has converted the simple presumption into definitive proof and has begun to deny political asylum to Spanish citizens, by allowing extradition.

Furthermore, before the implementation of the new policy, in September 1984, the Spanish Government had brought pressure to bear on the French authorities to expel certain Basque refugees.Wanting at the same time to avoid outright scandal, which would have followed expulsions, they brought in a new law which allowed for deportation to other countries which were willing to co-operate with them in the interests of good relations with France and Spain. Spain also took part in this operation, by indemnifying these countries and by paying for the deportees' transport and subsistence.

This policy of deportation took a form that was indefensible from a legal point of view. The deportee, once delivered to another country, was neither a prisoner, nor a refugee, nor a tourist, nor a citizen of any kind. Without legal status and deprived of all legal protection, refugees were subjected to all kinds of arbitrary decisions: just as in the case of the two deportees tortured with electrodes by the Spanish police in Equador. With a few exceptions the same happened to those who were deported to Cuba — interminable delay in dealing with their cases and abuse of the worst kind. In these circumstances, and contrary to the principles of law, 50 Basque refugees were deported between January 1984 and May 1989. They are still in the countries to which they were sent: Cape Verde, Cuba, Panama, the Dominican Republic, Sao Tomé in West Africa, and Venezuela.

For the French State, deportation was a half-way measure between refusing to hand over Basque refugees, before 1984, and the first extraditions in September of that year. Once begun, deportation continued in spite of the change in French strategy, which consisted of extraditions both legal and illegal. This change of attitude on the part of the French Government, starting in 1984, went hand-in-hand with a fresh spate of prison sentences, banning orders in the

départements of southern France, and the enforced residence of
Basque refugees. These measures were already in operation to some
extent but from this time on they became very common. Enforced
residence means that a person has to live in a specified French town
or *département* which he is not allowed to leave without official
permission. All these measures have for long been taken against
Basque refugees and they are still in force today.

After the deportations which began in January 1984 and the
extraditions beginning in the following September, the attitude of the
French authorities worsened and a policy of expulsion was now
implemented. There is an important difference between expulsion
and extradition. Whereas the latter requires a judicial process, expulsions do not have to go before a tribunal and can take the form of a
simple administrative procedure. They are put into effect by the
handing over of refugees by the French police to the Spanish,
without any other formalities and without any judicial involvement.
This new measure was put into force following the victory of the
French Right at the legislative elections of March 1986. At the time,
the new French Government (which succeeded the Socialist Governments in place since May 1981, with Mitterand still President) asked
its Spanish counterpart to put an end to the para-police activities of
GAL (*Grupos Antiterroristas de Liberación*), to which we shall come
later, offering in exchange the direct expulsion of Basque refugees
without going through judicial procedures. Most of the two hundred
or so, expulsions carried out between July 1986 and May 1988 were
in the 'extremely urgent' category and were arranged under a law
dating from the 1940s which had been drafted in a quite different
spirit, since it was meant for people who were thought to be a serious
and imminent danger to the French State.

If people in the northern Basque Country had been deeply off-
ended and even terrorized during the period 1984-86, mainly by the
escalation of *GAL* activity on its territory, their indignation grew
even more intense in 1986 when the new form of collaboration
between the French Government and the Spanish police became
known.

The first expulsions of July 1985 prompted a protest by 60 elected
Nationalists in the northern provinces against ' the handing over of
refugees to the Spanish police, whose use of torture has been condemned again this year by Amnesty International' and against 'police
control within the French State over magistrates who alone are
entitled to make decisions'.

In the same month, an important group of Nationalists and
sympathisers launched a campaign under the slogan 'one refugee,

one home', in order to obtain lodgings for Basque refugees. This campaign was given an extraordinarily warm reception, thanks to the good relations which have always existed between refugees and the people of the northern provinces, and also to their indignation at the growing collaboration of the French with police torture and para-police methods in Spain. In August, a group of elected representatives in the northern Basque Country made a new statement against the 'extremely urgent' measures. Four councillors and twelve mayors took part in a press-conference, despite the fact that the decision had been taken at the last minute. They included Nationalists, two Communists and even a Socialist, as well as a former M.P. and Vice-President of the General Council of Pyrénées-Atlantiques. Several lawyers representing Basque refugees also attended.

The Amnesty International report for October 1986 to March 1987 was a shot across the bows of the French Government about the 50 expulsions which had already taken place: 'Amnesty International's point of view on these expulsions is that nobody should be sent from one country to another where he might reasonably be expected to be tortured.' The French Government was also asked 'to obtain credible guarantees from the Spanish Government that it will not use its anti-terrorist laws against those who are expelled, which in the opinion of this organization can lead to torture.' The second part of the report, for the period from April to September 1987, goes on: 'Amnesty International is opposed to the expulsion of Basques from France to Spain because, in its view, there are good reasons for thinking that they could be subjected to torture. Article 3 of the UN Convention against Torture makes it clear that no State can expel, hand over or extradite a person to another State where this is presumed to be the case.

'This Convention was ratified by France on 18 February 1986. Amnesty International has expressed its concern about these expulsions, to both the French and Spanish Government, since the implementation of the new policy in July 1986. Its concern was due to the serious and well-documented complaints of torture and other abuses inflicted in some of these cases.' The report concludes by demanding that those about to be expelled should be dealt with by the Spanish judges and not the police, that they should be able to choose their own lawyers and that verdicts should not be too long delayed. All this is proof that Amnesty International knows what it is talking about.

In May 1988 there came another change of Government in France and the Socialist Pierre Joxe replaced the right-wing Minister of the Interior, Charles Pasqua. This put an end to the expulsions considered to be 'extremely urgent', but yet more expulsions took place with the introduction of a new procedure known as 'returning to the frontier', which once again consisted of handing over refugees by one police force to the other. As soon as the Right was once again returned to office in France, the procedure of 'extreme urgency' was re-established, so that it can be said today that both types of expulsion, by the judiciary and the police, are in operation simultaneously. The choice of procedure in any case is purely arbitrary.

Para-police activities

Whenever a Government wants to put down a determined popular movement, it has recourse to illegal methods and, as we have already seen, the anti-democratic position which refuses self-determination gradually reaches the point where it has to torture detainees. It also has to go in for inhuman treatment of political prisoners and the sanctioning of undercover activities by para-police groups. All these factors are connected and can only be explained together. There can be no partial explanations. We might think that the Spanish Government takes pleasure in having recourse to illegal methods: because of the precautions it has to take, the risks that it is always running, the fear from one moment to the next that its blood-stained hands will be exhibited in public. The Government would no doubt prefer to operate legally, but the effective working of the police precludes it. The police authorities obviously refuse to admit defeat in advance and a moment arrives when they demand action that is 'effective and without restrictions'. This implacable logic has been observed in relations between European powers and their colonies in the Third World. Even if the relationship between the Basque Country and the Governments in Madrid or Paris is not quite that of a classic colony, since the country's sovereignty is being denied and there is popular resistance, the use by these Governments of illegal methods is more a matter of circumstance than of principle.

The use of illegal methods on the part of a State does not always arise from Nationalist grievances. They can also be used to combat other movements such as Green groups, as we saw when François Mitterand decided to allow the use of explosives against 'Rainbow Warrior' in New Zealand. Each time a State takes up an anti-democratic position against a popular movement (be it national or some other kind), it eventually becomes caught up in a spiral which requires undercover action. During the ensuing struggle there always arrives a moment at which the use of armed force (whether by the army or police) will become a necessity.

The covert activities carried out by the agents of a State have their root cause in a negation of the people's rights, which in certain conditions leads inexorably to secret operations. Repression is usually preceded by a distortion of democracy, by a form of political perversion. The Spanish State has at various times organized para-police activities against the Basque movement and the French State has lent some of these activities its discreet backing. Under Franco, the Spanish State started to use illegal methods by torturing detainees, but it hardly ever beat up prisoners and it did not organize para-police goups with a view to eliminating its enemies. Of these three illegal methods, we can say that it was Franco who introduced torture (in 1939), the *UCD* which created para-police groups (beginning in late 1975), and the *PSOE* which initiated the beating of prisoners (in 1982).

In the Basque Country those who carry out attacks on militants are usually described as 'out of control'. It would seem that this term has its origins in an official explanation that 'uncontrolled elements' are responsible for the actions of the extreme Right. It is a term that has a certain irony in an everyday context because everyone understands that it refers to mercenaries who are in fact very well controlled. That is why the expression is usually written in inverted commas. The first 'uncontrolled' incidents actually took place before the advent of the *UCD* Government, although it was this party which was responsible for promoting them until they became quite commonplace. In October 1975, while Franco was still alive (he was to die a month later), a group of Civil Guards — according to eye-witnesses — killed a member of a Basque militant family named Etxabe on his business premises in the southern part of the country. There had been several unsuccessful attacks before this time. But from this date on, para-police groups crossed the frontier from Bidasoa more and more frequently in order to attack Basque refugees. They created such an embarrassing situation for the French Government that Poniatowski, the Minister of the Interior, told the National Assembly on 4 June 1975: 'Certain deplorable facts have recently come to light. Spanish police have been crossing incognito on to French soil. I have demanded of the Spanish authorities that the necessary diplomatic steps be taken so that these agents are prevented from carrying out their mission in France.'

In 1976, in the northern provinces, there were eight explosions, one kidnapping and three deaths. The attacks resulted in a number of people being injured. The French police arrested a Spanish citizen whose van was found to be loaded with guns, ammunition and a number of documents relating to Basque refugees. However, through the intervention of the Spanish Consul in Bayonne he was set free. In May several Spanish and Italian activists attacked a Carlist gathering in Montejurra in Navarra, causing two deaths and injuries. The Italian Carlo Ciccutini, who had sought refuge in Franco's Spain while on the run from persecution in his own country, admitted to 'having worked with Spanish security forces in their operations in France with the group known as *ATE* (*Anti Terrorismo ETA*) by spying on members of the Left and *ETA* and by taking part in attacks against the latter.'

The activities of those said to be 'out of control' were sometimes so intense and frequent during the years of political transition that there were times when they were beginning to terrorize whole communities and districts. Towards the end of 1978 the para-police organization known as *Batallon Vasco Español* (Spanish Basque Battalion) arrived on the scene. It carried out numerous attacks against Basque militants on both sides of the frontier and sometimes against the civilian population.

Such was the tension created by this organization that Giscard d'Estaing, at the time President of the French Republic, was reported as saying on 6 October 1979: ' It is intolerable that the Spanish police come on to French territory in order to settle their accounts.' Five days later, Manuel Fraga Iribarne, leader of the Spanish Right, made a rather different statement: ' I am in favour of police co-operation, which has borne such good results in France.' A short while earlier, on 30 July 1979, Ramón Rubial, President of the Socialist Party, declared in much the same spirit: 'There is one way of liquidating *ETA* and that is the way used by France against the *OAS* in Algeria, a formidable organization in which some high-ranking individuals were implicated. But no democracy can admit as much.' Whereas in France the Spanish intervention provoked unease, the main political leaders in the south began openly to express support for para-police activities.

In 1980 a number of young women not known to be militants were raped in various parts of the southern Basque Country, all apparently the victims of the same para-police group: the rapists carried guns, acted in concert, and interrogated the women about their political opinions and about *ETA*. The daily newspaper *Deia,* the organ of the *PNV,* wrote in its issue for 19 September 1980: 'During the course of the last five years, the extreme Right has carried out 500 attacks in the Basque Country, resulting in a total of 38 people being killed and 128 injured. In the north, 15 members of these units have been detained, while in the south only four junior members have been arrested.'

In November 1980 a Basque couple involved in a committee that was helping prisoners and refugees in Venezuela were killed in Caracas. A few days later, several armed men entered a bar in Hendaye, just inside the northern Basque Country, and fired on the customers, killing two local men. The gunmen managed to escape but were arrested at the frontier by the Spanish police who, acting on orders from a higly placed officer, promptly set them free. The police later admitted that the gunmen were anti-*ETA* informers and refused to give their names to the judge. The French police discovered that the bullets fired on this and other occasions matched those used by the Spanish police. The French Minister of the Interior, Christian Bonnet, accused the Spanish police of complicity in these murders, saying on 26 November 1980: 'Despite requests by the French police at the frontier post at Hendaye, the Spanish police refused to hand over the fugitives and reveal their identities to their counterparts. The French Government cannot accept such behaviour which seems to us to amount to complicity.'

The initials used by those described as 'out of control' have varied from time to time. Between 1975 and 1980 there were seven victims whose deaths were said to be the work of *ATE* (the anti-*ETA* group) or groups using some other name; we include in this category an attack against the Etxabe brothers, already mentioned, and the killing of the well-known leaders of *ETA,* Pertur and Argala. Between 1977 and 1980 three more deaths occurred for which a group calling itself *Triple A* claimed responsibility. In 1979 a killing was carried out by a group calling itself *ANE* and, in 1979/80, a group with the initials *GAE* claimed six more.Between 1979 and 1981 the name *BVE* (*Batallón Vasco Españonl*) was used by a group claiming 22 more killings. Once the *PSOE* had come to power, it was *GAL* which, between October 1983 and February 1986, claimed 26 killings, most of them in the northern provinces. A twenty-seventh person was killed by *GAL* in July 1987, but it seems that this murder was not carried out on orders from the group's leaders. Lastly, there was the death in 1989 of the *Herri Batasuna* M.P., Josu Muguruza, in the Hotel Alcalá in Madrid, a carefully planned attack, which was apparently carried out by yet another para-police group.

The Basques have always had the impression that all these various initials did not really correspond to any actual organization, but that they were really only names that had been concocted in order to mask para-police activity. This impression was finally confirmed during an interview with Luis Cervero Carrillo, a sergeant in the Civil Guard, which was published in the magazine *Interviú.* 'The group known as *ATE*,' said the officer, 'was a mixed group made up of Civil

Guards and extremists. The group had no organization as such. It was one of the many acronyms invented and used by groups receiving orders from the Civil Guard's High Command.' According to the *EFE* press-agency, a member of *GAL* claimed in June 1985 that ' acting on orders from the *UCD*, we were expected to carry out attacks under the name *Batallón Vasco Españonl (BNV)* and now we do the same under the name *Grupos Antiterroristas de Liberación* (Anti-terrorist Liberation Groups). But the fact is that, behind these two names, we are the same people'.

GAL

Although we have seen that para-police operations against Basque militants were first put in hand by Governments of the Spanish Right (*UCD*), the most important and the best-known of these activities, which were carried out by *GAL*, correspond strictly to the period when the *PSOE* was in power. Before the party took office in October 1983, just one year after its electoral victory, there had been no para-police activity for more than two years.

On 15 October 1983, in Bayonne, late in the afternoon, two young Basque refugees from Tolosa were visiting another group of refugees. This was to be the last time they would see one another. The two young people disappeared and were never heard from again. The complaints made by their companions proved in vain. The two refugees had joined 'the disappeared'. The Government in Madrid had once again decided to fight 'a dirty war'. It was discovered much later, during the questioning of a *GAL* member on 5 March 1985, that they had been taken away in a boat by two members of this para-police group. They had then been tortured to death in exchange for a large sum of money that the Spanish police officer José Amedo was to pay the group.

Four days later, on 19 March, under orders from the same police chief in Bilbao, Francisco Álvarez, who was later to be suspected of being the founder of *GAL*, a group of policemen in Hendaye tried to kidnap a leader of one of the *ETA* cells. The operation failed because the refugee put up a fight which led to the arrest of the four agents by the French police. Álvarez told the Spanish judge that he had organized the operation 'for humanitarian reasons', in order to exchange the Basque for a militia-man who was being held by *ETA*. He refused to appear before the French judge, needless to say.

These two incidents — the murder of the two young refugees and the attempted kidnapping — can be considered as the first operations carried out by *GAL*, even if the initials did not appear as such until a third attack, namely the kidnapping on 4 December 1983 of Segundo Marey, a man from the northern part of the country, whom *GAL* is believed to have mistaken for someone else. Be that as it may, Marey (as was learned later) was taken under cover across the border and handed over to the Spanish police (that is, José Amedo) in the presence of Civil Guards and then interrogated about Basque refugees. He reappeared on the northern side of the border ten days after being taken away, and a few hours after the setting free of four policemen arrested on suspicion of the aforementioned kidnapping. The incident was claimed by a hitherto unknown organization, namely *Grupos Antiterroristas de Liberación*, or *GAL,* in a communiqué which read as follows: 'In view of the growing number of murders, extortions and kidnappings carried out by *ETA* on Spanish soil, but planned and directed from France, we have decided to put an end to this situation. Each and every killing by *ETA* will henceforward be avenged.' In addition to this declaration of principle, the communiqué tried to explain the release of Marey: 'As a sign of goodwill and gratitude for the gesture of the French Government (who had liberated the four Spaniards) we are prepared to set Segundo Marey free. He was arrested by our organization because of his involvement with the terrorists of *ETA.*'

A few days after the release of the kidnapped Hendaye man, the French police arrested a Spanish ex-legionnaire, upon whom they found 35 photographs of Basque refugees bearing their personal details, all of which had been directly provided by the Spanish police and, more specifically, by Commissar Álvarez, whose telephone number was written on several of them. Of the 35 refugees, 28 were to fall victims of *GAL* bullets between October 1983 and February 1986, at which time this para-police activity came to an end.

In December 1983, *GAL* claimed its first victim in the northern part of the country. There followed a long list of deaths and injuries which were caused by attacks carried out in systematic fashion. These attacks were, as a general rule, so well-prepared and successful that the public began to realize that they must have been co-ordinated. The Spanish police would provide the exact name and description of the refugee, the French police his address and details of his daily routine, and with the help of this information the mercenaries would then carry out the killing of their victim. The complete absence of police inquiries, on both the French and Spanish side of the border, seemed to confirm the public's suspicions. The timing and information gathered about these attacks would show, in due course, that there was a pattern to them. The actions of *GAL* gave rise, from the outset, to demonstrations and protests in the

Basque Country, and these soon degenerated into violent confrontations with the police. In those districts where the victims had lived, the public's reaction was almost unanimous, and there were many general strikes, both local and regional.

Early in 1984, in its numbers for January and February, the magazine *Euskadi*, published by the *PNV*, carried a list of *GAL*'s personnel which pointed directly at the Spanish Government as the instigator of the attacks. Also in February the Spanish magazine *Tiempo* published the following statement by an expert on *ETA*: 'Unlike previous attempts, *GAL* represents an all-out struggle, both direct and psychological, and it has political objectives which have a bearing on the whole of the Basque Country.'

GAL has not always been successful. It has made mistakes, naturally. Those who killed, in error, a French railway-worker in the frontier station of Hendaye, in March 1984, and were then arrested by the Spanish police, claimed to be members of *GAL*. Shortly afterwards, the Vice-President of the Spanish Government, Alfonso Guerra, made an absolutely astonishing statement about his knowledge of *GAL,* in which he said: 'These were individuals who were trying to get into *GAL* but who did not in fact belong to that organization.' In the same month, the Algerian Jean-Pierre Cherid, one of *GAL*'s most prominent mercenaries (who had also worked with the *BVE*), was killed in action. His death forced the French police to arrest several of his comrades, but they were soon set free 'because of irregularities in their arrest'. The identity-card which Cherid was carrying at the time of his death bore the name of a Madrid man whose documents had been confiscated by the Civil Guard a little earlier. The mercenary's widow received a life-pension from the Spanish Ministry of the Interior.

But towards the end of 1984, *GAL* decided on a course of action that was different from what had gone before. The weekly newspaper of the *PNV*, *Euskadi,* in its edition for 20 December 1984, expressed the view that this initiative was part of a wider campaign against insurgents, which it described thus: ' In the struggle against guerrillas led by the security forces of countries such as Britain, Israel, South Africa, and Peru, methods similar to those now being adopted by the Spanish State have long been used.'

On 20 November 1984, the paediatrician Santiago Brouard, one of the leaders of *Herri Batasuna,* was killed in his surgery in Bilbao, just as he was about to examine a baby. The attack was claimed by *GAL* which up to then had confined its activities to the north. The death of this tireless Basque patriot, who had friends among *ETA* members, was unanimously condemned by all political parties and

by the Spanish Government, which announced that it was 'determined to bring to justice whoever had committed this terrible
crime.'

After many obstructions had been overcome and many years had
gone by, the judges in the case being continually replaced, this crime
— like so many others of its kind — was investigated but never
solved. Only one man was accused, as if he had acted on his own,
despite the fact that the doctor's nurse had recognized the man who
accompanied him: he was someone who had been working for the
Comisario General de Información. Another witness had also identified a second man, named Rafael Masa, who managed to flee from
Spain with the aid of false documents provided by a lieutenant in the
Civil Guard. Brouard's death provoked a general strike throughout
the southern Basque Country during which the largest crowd ever
seen demonstrated outside the Town Hall of Bilbao.

In April 1985 the daily paper *Le Monde* carried a story about *GAL*
in which it revealed connivance between Cherid, the Algerian mercenary, and the Civil Guard in Bilbao. The magazine *Euskadi* ran a
feature entitled 'On the Trail of *GAL*' in its number for 18 April 1985
which concluded thus: '*GAL* is one more element of an anti-terrorist
strategy being implemented by certain sectors of the Spanish State,
a part of a carefully prepared campaign against the insurgents, and
copied from other countries with which those responsible have contacts. The last step towards the 'normalization' of the Basque Country looks like being a civil confrontation brought about by sectarian
attacks and a psychological war of Sibylline proportions.'

One of the most serious of *GAL*'s attacks was that carried out by
several of its members in September 1985 in a Bayonne bar fre-
quented by Basque refugees, which resulted in eight deaths and many
injuries. Two members of the gang were arrested shortly afterwards
and, while they and other mercenaries were held in detention, it
became clear, in even more convincing ways, that those who were
running this 'dirty war' were based in Madrid. But the Government
in Paris did not seem to feel the same indignation as it had on
previous occasions. The Prime Minister, Laurent Fabius, gave an
assurance in a television interview broadcast in April 1986 that the
idea of physically eliminating Basque militants on their own ground
did not surprise him: 'I have never taken such a decision but, had it
proved necessary, I would have taken it.'

On the other hand, at about the same time, concern was being
expressed by the French media. The television programme *Magazine,* using the significant title 'Dirty Hands', broadcast an hour-long
report on *GAL.* After showing the grisly results of the attacks carried

out by this group in the northern Basque Country, the programme interviewed several police officers and mercenaries who directly implicated the Spanish State. Three days later this programme was shown on Basque television , but it was never broadcast in Spanish, on either Basque or Spanish television.

The report began by describing the difficulties encountered by the makers of the programme: ' We asked for an interview with the Commissioner of Police in Biarritz but the Ministry of the Interior forbade it. The same thing happened when we approached the police in Bordeaux, Pau and Bayonne. At the highest levels the Ministry of Justice and the French police refused to co-operate in this report. We are entitled to ask why.' This was a most pertinent question, as time would show. The journalist Santiago Aroca, from the magazine *Tiempo,* taking part in the programme, said that since the beginning of his enquiries about *GAL* he had encountered 'many legal problems and all sorts of complications and delicate situations. I do not want to sign my own death-warrant and I am not made of the stuff of heroes. My paper decided to send me to Brussels as an EEC correspondent'.

When, after overcoming several real difficulties, the interviewer managed to speak to police officer González Pacheco, a specialist in torture under Franco and suspected of being one of the organizers of *GAL*, the latter said: 'I am only carrying out orders. Go and see the King, the Minister of the Interior. I am only paying for the mistakes of my superiors.' The programme also showed an interview with José Luis Espinosa, who was described as 'a former collabora-tor with the Spanish secret services and the *Batallon Vasco Español'.* He said: 'In the *BVE* and in *GAL* everything is done as in other para-police groups. Like, for example, under De Gaulle with the *SAC (Service Action Civique)*, or with the *barbouzes* (secret police) in Algeria. The secret police all over the world function according to the same principle, which consists of paying mercenaries and inform-ers, even criminals, for their services.

'As for what has been happening recently, I can't say, for there are never more than three or four people who are in the know at any one time: those who are going to carry out the operation or who plan it with me. You call them "attacks" but for us they are "operations". You may argue about it, but no — don't smile — this is how it is. For us it's an "operation", a "job".' The French journalist added, 'A dirty job?', to which Espinosa replied, 'No, the dirt belongs to the State that pays us.'

The Civil Guard José Luis Cervero Carillo was another of the police officers interviewed. He said: 'Barrionuevo has, as his boss, an officer from the Civil Guard whose name is Manuel Pastrana Griñón and who, under Franco, was in the undercover police force. Today he is in charge of *GAL*, assisted by his immediate superior officer, Captain Félix Hernando, and by Cassinello and Santamaria and with Barrionuevo's approval. I know González Pacheco. We took part together in an operation against members of *GRAPO* in La Coruña. To my knowledge, he is now a member of *GAL*. He organizes para-police groups.' The journalist then asked, 'For whom does he work?' The policeman replied, 'For the Ministry of the Interior. He works there officially. He works with the special services. It was Pastrana Griñón himself who told me this.'

The last 'out of control' policeman to be interviewed on the French television programme preferred to remain anonymous but admitted that he worked in the Intelligence service. To the question, 'What exactly is *GAL*?', he replied: 'When the new Ministry of the Interior team and the Socialist Minister took charge of the anti-terrorist campaign, all the people working with them were the same ones as before. They were given a free hand in the fight against *ETA* and told that they could use any method whatsoever. It was then that *GAL* made its first apparently mysterious appearance. In fact, it did not appear mysteriously. It was created by the police, who recruited several former members of the *BVE* and some of their associates, and then started everything up again.'

To the question: 'Who was it really brought *GAL* into being? Can you give us the names of a few people inside the Government?', the policeman replied: ' As far as the Government is concerned, *GAL* was formed within the security forces, to which all the police chiefs belong. Among those who take part in its deliberations are General Cassinello, the Head of Intelligence, the Director of State Security who at the time was Rafael Vera, and one of the men who worked with the police chief, Francisco Álvarez Sánchez, who was very close to Conesa. It was Sánchez who gave the group its name and its initials.'

After showing interviews with Sánchez and his boss Julián San Cristóbal, the last part of the programme came back to Juan Alberto Belloch, who a few years later, in 1993, was to be appointed Minister of Justice and then Minister of the Interior. He said: 'The only collective involvement in all this was that of the Ministers of the Interior, and it is still a closely knit fraternity. The impression I have is that this cohesion exists not only despite political differences but also despite differences between countries. It is something shared by many Ministries and Intelligence Services. What's more, it's difficult to know where one begins and the other ends. In France the silence of the authorities is significant. There is an understanding, an obvious complicity with what goes on.'

The statements by the Director of State Security, Julián San Cristóbal, who tried to claim that there was no link between the Spanish police and *GAL*, prompted Charles Pasqua, the French Minister of the Interior, to say in May 1986: ' We disapprove completely of intrigues taking place on French soil, in defiance of the law, by people paid by a foreign State to settle its scores on our territory.'

Since the beginning of the *GAL* campaign in the northern Basque Country there has been no lack of support for refugees. In October 1985 there was a Solidarity March which went through many districts in the north. But among French intellectuals who, decades earlier, had been prepared to speak up on humanitarian grounds, there are few today willing to break the silence surrounding the two Socialist Governments in the face of the *GAL* atrocities. Among exceptions to this rule is the French lawyer and writer Denis Langlois. Four years later he would receive the Human Rights Prize from the hands of Laurent Fabius who, as an ex-Minister, had made the serious allegations to which we have already referred. Just after taking part in the Solidarity March, Langlois wrote of the Basques: 'I have eaten at their tables, I have slept under their roofs, I have talked with them, and my heart has been filled with hope. I have discovered a real community, not one of those folkloric things that are put on show in museums — a living community, with its own language and an ancient culture that looks forward to tomorrow. This is a people among whom solidarity, friendship and brotherhood are not mere words. This is a community which closes ranks in the face of danger, but in which people sing and dance not only for sheer enjoyment but also out of a profound feeling that they are alive.'

Since it was formed, *GAL* has killed no fewer than 27 people, and injured many more. The average of one killing per month, a high figure, suggests the involvement of several dozen participants and the availabilty of substantial funds. The end of its activities coincided with the electoral triumph of the French Right in the elections of March 1986, which marked the beginning of a new phase of co-operation between the French and Spanish States. The newly elected Government, as we have already explained, asked the Spanish authorities to stop the activities of this sinister group, offering in exchange, directly and without any judicial procedures, to hand over as many Basque refugees as it desired. And thus it turned out. After February 1986 the group took action on only one more occasion, causing the death of Juan Carlos García Goena. Given that official agreement had already been reached, this killing was assumed to have been carried out by an individual acting alone, namely the police officer José Amedeo Fouce, the group's worst offender. To all intents and purposes, *GAL* had given up in March 1986 when the new French Government took office.

Since the calling off of the *GAL* offensive there have been no further para-police activities. It may be that plans were conceived in certain quarters, and that some were even put in hand, but be that as it may, they were not carried out as part of a murderous campaign as previously.

The attack in the Hotel Alcalá in Madrid on 20 November 1989 was an isolated incident, unrelated to anything previous to it or since. What happened was that as the four newly elected *Herri Batasuna* M.Ps, who had decided to take their seats in the *Cortes* on the day following, were dining together in the hotel, two paid killers walked into the restaurant and shot the young M.P. and journalist Josu Muguruza and seriously injured his fellow-M.P., the lawyer Iñaki Esnaola. The date chosen for the killing might be thought to have symbolic significance: 20 November 1936 was the day that the leader of the Spanish Falange, José Antonio Primo de Rivera, was shot and, by coincidence, the day on which Franco died in 1975. But it may not have been a coincidence that 20 November was the date chosen for the killing of the two *Herri Batasuna* leaders, Santiago Brouard in 1984 and Josu Muguruza in 1989.

Josu Muguruza, a refugee in the northern Basque Country since the end of 1981, had been handed over to the Spanish police under the 'extremely urgent' procedures of March 1987, after which he was gaoled for six months. Early in 1988 he began working for the newspaper *Egin*, as chief sub-editor. Having joined the directorate of *Herri Batasuna* in May of that year, he was elected a Member of the Madrid Parliament in the elections of October 1989. The fact that he had been a political refugee and therefore might have had contacts with members of *ETA*, together with his important role on the staff of *Egin* and as a leading member of *Herri Batasuna*, had made him a vital part of the Basque movement. But since he did not have a high public profile, we can be sure that only the police or their agents would have singled him out as a target.

When it came to give an account of this attack, the Ministry of the Interior went to great pains in claiming that Muguruza had been shot 'by accident', which was not at all borne out by the bullets' trajectory. Be that as it may, the assassination was followed by one of the largest demonstrations in the recent history of the Basque

Country. The President of the Government in Vitoria said: 'The shooting which has taken place in the Hotel Alcalá could have the gravity and importance of a crime committed by the State.'

The man chosen to hold an inquiry into this incident had been a police inspector during the Franco era. What is more, the bullets used to kill Muguraza were of the same type as those used by the Army. Also, two members of the Civil Guard's intelligence unit had been keeping an eye on the Basque M.Ps from a nearby table. The men who were brought to trial, a long time afterwards, were a policeman and the son of a well-known Army officer who had taken part in several attempted coups d'état. The first of these was found guilty and the second given an absolute discharge. Against all the evidence, they were said to have had neither bosses nor accomplices. Earlier inquiries had singled out several people from the Ministry of the Interior and the Civil Guard.

Unlike in the trials of Basque political prisoners, at which the only evidence is usually provided in statements made by the detainee while in solitary confinement, in this particular case the trial took account only of the oral statements made during the proceedings, ignoring all the contradictions which had come to light during the earlier hearings. It is clear that the policeman accused of injuring the lawyer was not acting alone, as several witnesses confirmed. Furthermore, the judge took the view that the accused had carried out the attack while he was off duty and, as a consequence, the State's complicity was never established in court. As for the shot that killed Josu Muguruza, no one was found guilty of firing it.

Extensive repression

In the preceding pages we have drawn attention to various aspects of the intensive measures designed to stifle the most combative section of the Basque population, the militants, with extreme harshness and without the slightest regard for life or limb. More extensive forms of repression are aimed at those parts of the population which, though disaffected, are not militant, and at the population as a whole. We shall here confine ourselves to the southern Basque Country and to a discussion of the policies implemented by the Government in Madrid, since the repressive policy of the French Government towards the Basques is less extensive and more selective.

The Basque Country, of all the territories within the Spanish State, has always suffered the greatest repression. During the course of the last century the reasons put forward were the Carlist Wars and the traditionalism of the Basque people which nourished them. In Franco's time, there was severe repression of the Basques in all spheres of life. Of the eleven states of emergency imposed by the Franco regime, five applied to the Basque provinces, another to the same provinces plus Asturias, another to the Asturias alone, and the remaining four to the whole of Spain. This may be a feeble enough indication of the Franco regime's attitude towards the Basques, but it is nevertheless significant. The same could be said for the period of transition under the Government led by the Spanish Democratic Right (the *UCD*). But we shall now deal with the period that corresponds to the mandate of the *PSOE*, and we shall begin by looking in particular at the *Plan ZEN*.

The Plan Zen

The *Plan ZEN* was set up by the *PSOE* just a few months after it took power. Its initials stand for *Zona Especial Norte*. This 'zone' refers to the four southern provinces of the Basque Country. Thus, ironically and for the very first time, the unity of the four provinces had at last been recognized, if only for police purposes. But at the same time, of course, the term 'north' concealed the specifically Basque purpose of the exercise. The *Plan ZEN* is in fact a police plan for the crushing of Basque dissidence, that is to say it is aimed at *ETA* and its allies, legal or illegal, practical or theoretical. The Plan is similar in outline to those contained in the counter-revolutionary manuals that used to be distributed by the United States after the end of the Second World War in its fight against Communism in Europe. It is concerned with reforming the police in order to make them more efficient in the fight against *ETA* and with developing new areas of propaganda such as psychological warfare and the spreading of disinformation. One of its objectives is to establish anti-*ETA* links with the trades unions, political parties, and all other kinds of associations with a view to breathing more energy into them and co-ordinating their activities. Another aim is to create a network of paid informers who will identify *ETA*'s sources of income and try to staunch them.

The Plan also aims at promoting media campaigns which try to show the incompatibility of *ETA*'s actions with traditional Basque values, pointing to their criminal character, their detrimental effects on property and people, and the negative consequences for the economy. It extols, on the other hand, what it sees as the positive aspects of police repression such as torture and other abuses. This Plan also supports the 'social rehabilitation' of militants, in imitation of the Italian model known as the Law for the Reformed Criminal, and demands that the police be better paid.

One of its characteristics is its scant respect for public opinion, as can be seen from the advice it gives: ' In all successful police operations, some of the credit should go to the co-operation of the public' . . . ; 'Whenever a policeman is the victim of an attack, identify him immediately, preferably providing details about his wife, mother and children' . . . ; 'Give information on a regular basis or through a third party about squabbles among terrorists, anything that reveals the foreign nature of their ideologies, their sordid deals, and so on.'

The *Plan ZEN*, from its inception, was proof that the new party in power, the *PSOE*, whether through lack of will or because it was incapable of taking more positive action, had decided at the outset to deal with the Basque problem by using the same police methods traditionally used by Madrid, without attempting to find any other perspective.

Public opinion

In its yearbooks the newspaper *Egin* publishes lists of demonstrations which have been prevented by the forces of public order. These usually contain details of various gatherings, rallies, and protests of all kinds which have not been allowed by the authorities. To read them is proof of the limited nature of democracy allowed by the Spanish State.

In the Basque Country the police are present at all kinds of meetings, whether they be of students, workers or ordinary people. Meetings are held in protest against the closure of factories, torture, the killing of militants, military service, police repression, deterioration of the environment, the drugs trade, immigration, the lack of housing, municipal and urban matters, union affairs, and so forth. All these in every other European country, with perhaps the exception of Turkey, are part of the people's democratic right to freedom of expression. In 1991 a total of 172 protests were broken up by the police, as were 120 in 1992 and 186 in 1993. The variety and extent of these protests are even more significant than their numbers and are unusually high for such a small country. Contrary to how they should be handled, the demonstrations do not all receive the same treatment from the police. One that is in favour of a certain proposed road-scheme will be tolerated and another obstructed, although even when the police do not use violence they will usually not be averse to hurling insults at demonstrators.

The Madrid Government always tries to prevent demonstrations which have a Nationalist character, whatever the reason for them may be. At the present time the principle of equality which should protect all citizens is set aside in almost every sphere of public life. Freedom of expression, and the right to publish and to receive information freely, are tampered with at all stages. Verbal and written communications which do not follow the official line suffer from harassment by the authorities. For example, access to information about institutions, an important source for an understanding of how the press and radio are run, is blocked. People who work in the media, members of the public and politicians are subjected to administrative and judicial persecution, even detention, for having expressed their views during the course of their work. As a consequence, municipal councillors, political leaders and militant Nationalists are dragged before the courts merely for having distributed propaganda in the street, for having taken part in public demonstrations, for having passed motions in the Town Halls, and so on. It is becoming more and more common for the legal representatives of Basque militants to be themselves caught up in the judicial process on account of their professional work.

The yearbooks published by *Egin*, to which we have already referred, also put on record instances of the infringement of freedom of expression, such as censorship, the closing down of premises, and the right to speak in public, which have taken place in the southern Basque Country recently. There were a total of 66 such cases in 1991, which went up to 85 in 1992 and 90 in 1993. Even more serious is the detention of people merely because of the opinions they have expressed. To be caught painting a slogan or sticking up posters or taking part in a meeting is enough to be detained by the police. The best-known case of detention was no doubt the imprisonment of the journalist Javier Sanchez Erauskin, who was given a year's sentence in 1983 for two offences connected with his work with a Nationalist magazine of which he had been editor for some years. He was sentenced the first time for having published an interview with the sisters of two Basque refugees, who had described their brothers as 'militants but not terrorists'. His second sentence was because he had written a satirical article which commented with tongue in cheek on the King's visit to Guernica in February 1981. They demonstrated with great clarity that the simple act of having expressed a contrary view is considered a criminal offence.

But public opinion is not altered simply by the suppression of divergent views. The authorities have a dishonest policy of making a travesty of the facts, ensuring that the media which they control, as well as those in the private sector which are most sympathetic to them for political and economic reasons, also distort them to suit the official line. There is no method of spreading disinformation which is not tried at one time or another: a subtle filtering process, the omission of a revealing fact, the over-exposure of an insignificant incident, the big lie, the broadcasting of news out of context, pure invention, the deliberate mistake, the simple speculation, the inappropriate analogy or metaphor, the wrong emphasis, the false rumour, the slight semantic fudge, caricature, the innocent euphemism, the generalization . . . Indeed, a detailed and systematic analysis of the language used in the media under the influence of the Spanish Government would be highly revelatory.

Other kinds of aggression

Besides those already noted, there are other kinds of persecution, which are just as extensive, such as aggression by para-police and police forces. The para-police activities of those said to be 'out of control' have already been dealt with. They include murders and attempted murders and other acts which have serious consequences, all directed against Basque militants. We are now going to touch upon some smaller matters which have less serious consequences but which affect a larger section of society. Three examples of this type which took place towards the end of 1990 were monitored by the newspaper *Egin*. First, on 25 November 1990, the doors of the house of Iñigo García in Martutene in Guipúzcoa and those of the *Taberna Berri* (a restaurant) were plastered with stickers which bore the words, 'Cowards, Murderers. *ETA*, no.' On 15 February 1990, unknown persons broke into the offices of the *LAB* trade union at Bermeo in Vizcaya, went through various documents and took away a small box containing a rubber stamp bearing the initials *LAB* and some membership cards. On 18 December 1990, *Herri Batasuna* in Llaudio in Álava complained about new threats to its members who had received anonymous telephone-calls in the small hours. They had also been spied upon and followed, and had received anonymous letters. A few months previously, the mayor and *Herri Batasuna* councillors had received suspicious parcels through the post. This kind of petty aggression has been common for some years now. In 1990 there were 30 such cases but more recently the number of reported incidents has gone down, which may mean a decline in para-police activity, at least for the moment.

As for police aggression in the stricter sense, it can be of two kinds: it can be committed by policemen during working-hours or else while they are off-duty. The latter kind, which cannot be

officially attributed to the police, are usually described as being the
work of those who are 'out of control'.

Four examples of police aggression, committed during working-
hours, in the latter half of 1993, were again monitored by *Egin.* On
24 September 1993, in the Rekalde district of Bilbao, a detachment
of National Police overturned a statue erected in memory of two
militants who had died under torture, and then defaced a mural
depicting this fact. On 27 September 1993, ten uniformed members
of the National Police stormed into the *Herriko Taberno,* a restaurant in the Santuxtu district of Bilbao, in pursuit of a group of
demonstrators. The policemen ransacked the premises, tore down
posters and demanded to see the identity papers of the customers,
mainly workmen who had no connection with the demonstrators.
On the same day, a policeman dressed in civilian clothes brandished
his revolver and threatened the *Herri Batasuna* senator José Luis
Elkoro and the M.P. José María Olarra as they were about to
approach a group of police officers to enquire about an arrest that
had just taken place in one of the streets of San Sebastián. The
policeman threw the senator's identity papers to the ground and
began threatening him with such phrases as 'You are all going to be
shot' and ' We'd kill you all if we could'. On 5 October 1993, several
young people had gathered in a Bilbao street during the visit of the
Spanish royal family. Among them were two youngsters who were
on their way to the *Museo de Bellas Artes* (Fine Arts Museum)
carrying a Basque flag. They were arrested by police officers who
forced them to take off the stickers they were wearing and swallow
them.

This kind of harassment and similar examples are going on all the
time in the Basque Country. About 70 cases were reported in the year
1993 and some 40 in 1992 and 1991. Sometimes the victims, who are
to a lesser or greater extent connected with the Basque movement,
are in sympathy with radical Nationalism, as in the above cases. At
other times, ordinary people, regardless of their beliefs, become
involved. There are altercations, for example, which are provoked
by policemen dressed as civilians in night-clubs, that is to say when
people are supposed to be enjoying themselves, and it can also
happen if you have the misfortune to pass by a group of tipsy
policemen in some lonely spot or other.

In view of the low esteem in which the Basque population hold
the police and the Civil Guard, the latter lead a somewhat miserable
life. They are unpopular in the street, in their own communities, and
while out shopping, and their children do not get on with those of
their neighbours. The rather paranoid reaction that ensues among

members of the police force has been called 'the Northern syndrome'; it includes various kinds of unbalanced behaviour and psychological disorders, such as extreme reaction to the slightest irritation, and in some cases it leads to suicide. Although the police receive a substantial increment for working in the Basque Country, a growing number have applied for transfer to zones elsewhere in Spain. But there are so many applications that they cannot all be processed at the same time. This tense situation is one of the factors that mar relations between Basques and the police. Just as the Spanish State blames its troubles on the Basque Country, working off its frustration in a quite hysterical fashion on the people of these provinces, at an individual level the police too perceive the Basques as the cause of their misfortunes and pour out their hatred upon them.

On the other hand, the struggle against persecution is one of the most widespread and long-standing in the Basque Country, and it prompts countless demonstrations and gestures of solidarity. As in previous chapters, a single but very general and representative example must serve: the most recent general strikes in protest against repression have been the following: 26 September 1984, against extraditions by France; 22 November 1984, against the killing by *GAL* of Santiago Brouard;18 December 1985, against the killing of Mikel Zabalza by the Civil Guard; and 22 November 1989, against the death in Madrid of the M.P. Josu Muguruza.

To understand the terrible impact of the Government's persecution of the population and the indignation that it causes, it should be borne in mind that these strikes were supported by the entire population of the four provinces. That is not to mention the many local strikes called in protest against repression in various districts or villages, nor those which received only partial support, but only those general strikes in which the whole population participated. This is a phenomenon of great significance which is not found in any other country in Europe.

The impunity of Spanish officials

The real problem is not that officials torture, kill and beat up prisoners, or that they commit serious fraud and perjury. Such appalling acts occur from time to time in democratic States. The situation is more serious when the State not only fails to combat such criminality but actually encourages it. Then the problem becomes very serious, because it is now absolutely certain that the evil will be repeated. How then does the Spanish Government react to a case of torture, or to the death of someone suspected of belonging to *ETA*?

By condemning it and trying to find out who did it? Or by trying to sweep it aside and even denying it altogether? If it reacted in the first way, democracy would be well served, even if the undercover operations carried out by officials really did occur. If it reacted in the second way, democracy itself would be in question.

Whenever an official's illicit deed is officially condemned, we can be sure that the initiative has definitely not come from above. When the deed is protected by the authorities, it means that the order has come from a higher echelon. As someone has written recently, 'In an occupied country, the law is always a dead letter'.

The newspaper *Deia*, published by the *PNV,* commented in an article on 14 February 1981: 'Every Government that turns a blind eye to death caused by torture is contaminated as much as the official who beats, mistreats or abuses his authority, for it brings the Constitution into disrepute, although it is supposed to guarantee the citizen's basic rights. Or is it that Fascism is not yet dead?' Next day the paper's editor, L.A. Aranberri, wrote: 'Really, it is difficult to see how a State that practises terrorism has the legal and moral capacity to denounce terrorism, and this lack of respect among the people can engender in society some pretty obnoxious disorders.'

The Spanish State's protection of those among its servants who commit illegal acts extends also to those who use torture, to those who follow a 'shoot to kill' policy when there is no need for it, to those who beat up prisoners, even to those who are crooks. Torture, as we have already said, makes sense only when it cannot be proven, for if it were proven, it would be quickly rejected by the public and not be repeated.

It is practically impossible to prove that someone has been tortured. Those guilty of it go to some lengths to protect their identity, covering their own faces and that of the detainee, leaving no marks, and taking great precautions which they have practised to perfection. That is why the method known as 'the hip-bath' is used, and electrodes. When the victim, emerging from his torment with the horror and pain of it still burning in his flesh, appears before the judge, he tries to describe what has happened. But the judge's impassive face, on which not the slightest emotion flickers, except irritation at having to listen once again to a terrifying tale that he has heard a thousand times before, conveys with great clarity the fate reserved for the accused. For the judges are indifferent, not only to these terrifying accounts but very often to the awful state in which the victims appear in the dock, with haematomas and injuries, trembling with delirium, sometimes almost incapable of speaking.

It is understandable that the Government does not want to lose

the services of a civil servant who has done his duty zealously
(especially since it could lead to a lack of recruits), but the fact
remains that official protection of torturers could not be more
evident than it is within the Spanish State, as the reports of Amnesty
International quoted in Chapter 6 amply demonstrate.

In the hundreds of cases in which torture is alleged a guilty verdict
is not very often returned. Out of that immense pile of complaints
filed in the courts in the last ten years or so, only six resulted in trials.
When a case does come up, which is not frequently, it is usually after
a delay of several years, in a chamber filled with police officers so
that there is no room for anyone else, and usually no one is found
guilty. It is highly likely that the Government grants special immun-
ity to those who commit torture on its behalf.

We may conclude by saying that torture within the Spanish State
is an offence which goes virtually unpunished, since it has been
denounced to no avail by a number of international bodies. As is
perfectly normal in these circumstances, the guarantee of impunity
extends not only to clandestine activities by civil servants, by which
we mean torture, but also to police officers, who must also be
protected against all possible incriminations. None of the many
killings to which we have referred has had any legal consequences
for those who carried them out. The first precaution taken by the
authorities is not to divulge their names to anyone. Neither the
policemen who 'shoot to kill', nor those who beat up Basque political
prisoners, nor those who take part in undercover police activities in
order to kill militants, have been found guilty. In this respect the
greatest insolence on the part of the Spanish authorities has been,
without any doubt, the protection of many officials who have participated in the operations of *GAL*, described above.

A series of open-and-shut cases in Portugal and France have led
to the trial of a number of *GAL* members and this pressure from
outside has persuaded the Spanish State to pretend to crack down
on this organization by putting two policemen up for trial, namely
José Amedo and Miguel Dominguez. Felipe González, in a statement on 29 July 1988 to journalists whose curiosity had been aroused
by a recent scandal, said quite explicitly : ' Despite the efforts of
certain people in this direction, it is not possible to demonstrate that
the State apparatus or its civil service has been implicated in the
activities of *GAL*.' A little while later he added: 'The State, run at
present by the Right, protects itself in the law-courts, but also in
drawing-rooms and gutters. When we are mature enough to understand that the gutter rules inside the edifice of the Right-wing State,
we shall have no need for further discussion.'

On 21 June 1990, Ramsey Clark, who had been Procurator General of the United States from 1963 to 1969, commented during a visit to Madrid: 'The Spanish Government is guilty of aiding and abetting *GAL.*' The lawyer and former Portuguese Minister José Sanchez Osorio said on 5 October 1991: ' I am sure that Barrionuevo and Felipe González knew all about *GAL*, although that was never proved.'

The trial of 'the Amedo case' in 1991 was a clear demonstration of the limits set by the Right-wing Government when it came to enquiries being made about the State apparatus. The judge Baltasar Garzón, in his diagram of *GAL*, which he drew up after making his own enquiries, put at the top of the pyramid an eloquent X, the true identity of whom has never been discovered. When the time came for a verdict, which seemed like something out of the Theatre of the Absurd, the two police officers seemed to have no bosses and no accomplices. This was despite many instances of proof of collaboration made public in the media and during the trials held in France and Portugal. As for the substantial sums invested in the murders, particularly for paying the mercenaries, nobody could work out where they had come from. If someone at a certain point in the proceedings had referred to the State's 'reserve funds', the authorities would have quickly declared that these funds, by their very nature, could not be the subject of an inquiry. The trial succeeded in reducing 'the *GAL* case' to 'the Amedo case'.

On 29 May 1996 a former chief of the Civil Guard, Luis Roldan, told the Supreme Court that Barrionuevo had informed him in 1990 that González knew about the *GAL* death-squads. Earlier that month the Court had cleared González of involvement in *GAL* but indicted Barrionuevo on charges of setting them up.

Chapter 8

SOCIAL MOVEMENTS AND
PARTICIPATORY DEMOCRACY

One of the characteristic features of Basque society is its highly participatory character. The country has always had an extraordinarily rich communal life, which is to be seen in the fields of sport, the arts, education, cuisine, religion, festivals, and in such recreations as hunting and fishing. This gregarious people can always find a good reason for forming a society or bringing together a group of people who share a common interest. It may very well be that this collective way of living and the interest the Basques show in social matters is part of the heritage of a mountain people in which mutual aid, which is often foreign to more liberal and individualistic traditions, is an indispensable condition for survival, but however that may be, it cannot be denied that this collective dimension is very strongly ingrained in the country's social life.

The Basque penchant for disputation in political matters would be incomprehensible if we were not aware of how they behave in other spheres that are not at all political, or at least, not strictly political. There have been numerous initiatives in recent decades for the solving of ecological problems, or other local matters, and even some of much wider scope.

Some of the main campaigns that have taken place since the political transition of the 1970s in turn date back to earlier campaigns started during the Franco regime. *ETA* was formed early in the 1960s and this organization has been of the utmost importance in the fight for the sovereignty of the Basque Country. At about the same time, two other important initiatives were taken that are not so well-known beyond our borders: the Basque-language schools and the co-operative venture at Mondragón.

In about 1960, in the district of Mondragón in Guipúzcoa, a co-operative movement was born which, within a few years, would become one of the most original and substantial branches of co-operativism in the world. This too reflects the strength of the traditional Basque custom of relying on one's own resources. At the present time, Mondragón employs about a fifth of the working population of the southern Basque Country, in both industrial production and the primary sector of the economy, and in the distribution and service sectors. This movement has spread throughout the whole of the country, encouraging among its people a certain egalitarianism which is also realistic in its general approach. Although it has a few weaknesses, the Mondragón co-operative is based on values that are deeply rooted in the psychology of those industrial, rural and semi-urban districts where it has come into being: dynamism, initiative, entrepreneurial flair, a genuine interest in work, a regard for organization and discipline, a sense of economy, a horror of waste, a sense of collectivity, a love of everything Basque, a regard for the highest standards in all things and a job well done, an independence of judgement, a scepticism about vertically organized structures, even a certain general mistrust, and a pragmatism lightly tinged with idealism.

Support for prisoners and those who suffer reprisals for political reasons has been another inexhaustible source of collective effort and public concern, and has led to the creation of various groups aiming to show solidarity and offer practical help. Among these are the *Gestora pro-Amnistia*, founded in 1976, and *Senideak*, founded in 1991, which for years now have worked tirelessly on behalf of those who suffer in the cause of Basque sovereignty, helping them to claim their rights and protect their often precarious financial situation. During the years of transition the campaign for an amnesty became the greatest source of popular protest, as seen during the famous 'Amnesty Weeks' and in other collective action of all kinds. It became so pressing at one point that the President of the *PNV*, Xavier Arzalluz, said on 19 March 1977: 'Amnesty will not come as a result of negotiation between politicians or parties and the Government, but only as a result of campaigning and public pressure.' There was an amnesty towards the end of 1977, some two years after the death of Franco, but only after there had been an enormous outcry.

The fight against drug-trafficking began in the late 1970s. At the time it had become clear that in the southern Basque Country the incidence of addiction was much higher than in other, less troubled parts of the Spanish State. Drugs tend to remove many young people from the political struggle and there are signs that the police play a part in peddling drugs, as much for this reason as to pay informers, and sometimes even for their own gain. Many anti-drug groups have been formed, such as *Proyecto Hombre* (1985) and *Askagintza* (1988), mainly among the families of addicts. Once again there has been a good deal of mutual aid, usually at the cost of great sacrifice on the part of these families, but the extent of this terrible evil has been much reduced in recent years. One of the *ETA*'s initiatives since 1980 has been precisely in this field: it often takes action against dealers, with the keen approval of the addicts' families.

Communal support for the Basque language

It was early in the 1960s that the schools known as *ikastolak*, to which we referred in Chapter 2, were first opened. These clandestine schools, which came into being during the heyday of the Franco regime, spread throughout the country and began teaching in a language that was thought to be in serious danger of extinction. They were set up in the southern provinces during the 1960s and in the north in the decade following. They have become so numerous during the 1990s that now one child in five, among those receiving compulsory education, is taught through the medium of Basque in the *ikastolak*.

These were private schools, the legal status of which has changed only recently, and they were set up and maintained by the considerable effort of thousands of families who, over many years, committed themselves generously to the cause of providing education for their children in Basque. They lent their financial support, held frequent meetings, taking risks and giving up much of their free time for this collective task of promoting the language. There is no comparable school system anywhere in Europe.

The schools have enjoyed the ongoing support of a large proportion of the population for their creation and maintenance. Of particular significance in this collective effort have been the annual festivals which have raised money for the *ikastolak*. Once a year, usually on a Sunday, each of the provinces puts on such a festival. The people organize a sponsored walk of several kilometres through one of the province's districts, in which sympathizers join or which they support with promises of money, and children's amusements are laid on as part of the day's attractions. There is a walk in each of the four southern provinces and a fifth in the north.

Whereas the *ikastolak* are devoted to the teaching of Basque to children, the *euskaltegi* (Basque language centres) teach it to adults. They teach those who have no previous knowledge of the language to speak it and those who can only speak it to read and write in it.

These are schools which aim at turning people into Basques, teaching them literacy in their own language. They rely in turn on a huge support network throughout the country. Like the *ikastolak*, they came into being as a direct response to the public's enthusiasm and commitment, especially to initiatives intended to help promote the language. As was pointed out in Chapter 2, these schools have been completely neglected by the authorities until recently, including those of the Autonomous Government which for many years has refused to encourage their valuable contribution to the nation's life. The reason for this neglect lies in the fact that many of the organizers of these schools hold political views which run counter to those of the Government. The schools for adults also organize their own annual festivals based on the idea of the sponsored walk. Teachers and pupils walk throughout the Basque Country, north and south, carrying banners and placards which every year symbolize the people's commitment to their language. These walks are known as the *Korrika*, which means 'on the move'.

It was in December 1990 that the first number of *Euskaldunon Egunkaria* (The Newspaper of all Basques), a paper written entirely in the language, made its appearance. The only precedent for this initiative was a paper published during the Civil War but that was of short duration. Once again, the effort needed to get it under way fell on the shoulders of several thousand individuals who, excited by this new departure for the language, lent it their financial and practical support. But in this instance too, just as with the schools that teach Basque to adults, and for the same reason, the authorities refused to lend their support, despite the fact that the paper is more open to a variety of opinions than any of the other existing publications. Like the *ikastolak* and the schools for adults, the newspaper's circulation takes in the whole country.

Among other initiatives worthy of note are the attempt to create, since 1989, a nucleus of municipalities which function through the medium of the language, the Summer University held through the medium of Basque, and the weekly paper *Argia*, all of which were mentioned at the end of Chapter 2.

Egin, an unusual experiment

The first number of *Egin* appeared at the end of 1977. It is one of the few examples in Europe of a newspaper that was created by a huge initiative on the part of its potential readership. Its launch was preceded by an intensive and extensive campaign, from village to village, partly aimed at explaining the need for a new, open-minded paper in Basque which would express left-wing Nationalist views, and partly to collect the funds necessary for setting it up. The paper's share-capital is fixed at a maximum number of *pesetas*, in order to prevent its being run by a restricted number of shareholders. More than 20,000 shares were bought initially and a further 10,000 in subsequent campaigns. The shareholders are represented at meetings in a collective way: those who can muster a million *pesetas* from among fellow-shareholders become delegates to the meetings.

The fact that it has no large shareholders gives *Egin* a very special character among newspapers in Europe: no shareholder is powerful enough to interfere in its editorial policy or to apply a veto or to insist that an article be published in the paper. This gives the editorial board a quite unusual freedom which allows it to deal, within legal limits, with such taboo subjects as police torture and corruption, and with other matters like the Basque language, national sovereignty, women's issues, the environment, and working conditions. The paper's existence has not only brought home to the public certain realities about life in the Basque Country but has also left its mark in an indirect but profound way on how the other media work. Without *Egin*, the other newspapers, radio stations and television channels would be able to ignore or slant items of news which do not please the authorities.

Another of its characteristics is the large number of appeals it has received from the public which draw attention, in no uncertain manner, to facts or versions of facts which would otherwise have been kept under wraps or been subject to shilly-shallying.

The authorities have tried very hard to make life difficult for this outstanding paper, by means of fines, a refusal to advertise in its pages, trials, confiscation of its property, and even threats of closure, but without success.

The campaign against the nuclear power station at Lemoiz

Opposition by the people to the nuclear power station at Lemoiz, in Vizcaya, is long-standing and has been extraordinarily consistent, mainly due to the fact that it has been associated with the armed struggle carried out by *ETA*. In the end the campaign was successful: this dangerous installation, situated within 17 kilometres of a popu- lation of about a million (Greater Bilbao), was brought to a halt in 1982 and then finally closed down in 1994, an occasion joyfully celebrated by the people of the region. The combination of public opposition and armed action resulted, perhaps more clearly in this case than ever before, in the realization of a deeply rooted popular will.

During the 1970s, the electricity generating company Iberduero planned four nuclear power stations in the southern Basque Country: the construction of those at Deba in Guipúzcoa and Tudela in Navarra was prevented by the respective 'provincial' authorities; nor was the one at Ipazter-Ea given the go-ahead, but construction of the reactor at Lemoiz, also in Vizcaya, started against a background of administrative irregularities, corruption and non-communication on the part of officialdom. In 1976 the Commission for the Protection of a Non-nuclear Basque Coast, together with a number of associations consisting of people who lived near the proposed site, mainly heads of families and representatives of cultural societies from the region affected, came out against the power station. They managed to gather 150,000 signatures in support of their point of view and organized mass-demonstrations, in several of which between 100,000 and 200,000 people took part. Soon the movement was joined by the Anti-nuclear Committees which succeeded in building up a solid and active network taking in the whole of the southern Basque Country. There were many more protests and demonstrations, and several fully documented dossiers were published on the subject of the power station which were signed by well-known practitioners in the arts and other prominent people. One of the artists, the sculptor Eduardo Chillida, designed a sticker protesting against the power station, which proved very popular.

The authorities refused to hold a referendum on the subject, for Prime Minister Suarez of the *UCD* would not allow it, claiming that the power station was the responsibility of the Government in Madrid. Soon, in 1977, the military wing of *ETA* entered the fray. During the course of the next few years it was to carry out some 300 attacks against installations belonging to the Iberduero enterprise. About a dozen people were killed in all — workers at the plant, some of the militants themselves, a few targeted victims and others who were killed by accident.

In 1979 there was a demonstration by some 20,000 protesters at the Lemoiz site. Setting out from Bayonne, the procession had gone through all the Basque provinces, gathering people on the way. A general electricity stoppage to many homes throughout the country was also arranged as a protest against the building of the power station, as well as a refusal to pay bills issued by Iberduero. The authorities' reaction to the campaign now seemed to suggest that it was no longer anything to do with Iberduero but more and more a matter for the State. In 1980 the site was declared a military zone. Then, early in 1981, *ETA* kidnapped one of the Iberduero engineers, who was also a director of the nuclear power station, and demanded the demolition of the plant in exchange for his life. The authorities refused and *ETA* killed the engineer, thus provoking a great commotion throughout the land. The Council of Ministers meeting on 15 January 1982 finally decided not to hold a referendum on the subject of the power station. Later in 1982 *ETA* killed another of the plant's senior employees, and this really put an end to the matter.

The campaign against the Lemoiz installation is a good example of the dichotomy that exists between Basque society as it exists on the ground and those who represent it politically. It was not merely an anti-nuclear campaign, for in the course of its development the campaigners were calling for Basque sovereignty. It also threw into high relief the political role played by the various social groups and their relationship to institutions, marked the limits of representative democracy as defined by the interests of the centres of economic power, and demonstrated the persuasive power of the armed struggle as carried on by *ETA*.

A democracy based on minority economic interests and on reasons of State is inconsistent with both a democracy that allows the people's participation and with a civil society's desire to take part in social and political life. But contradictions so deeply rooted in our society emerge only when there are specific cases, like that of Lemoiz, which have widespread and tenacious popular backing.

A short while after paralyzing the Lemoiz plant, *ETA* drew its own conclusions in an interview published in September 1982 in the magazine *Enbata*. It said that the aim of its armed intervention was to ensure 'that the Basques should regain a modicum of democracy which will allow them to govern themselves and, in particular, to ensure freedom of speech, so that they might also have political freedom in a form consonant with their own way of life and well-being'.

The Basque 'no' to NATO

Basque opposition to the Spanish State's membership of the North Atlantic Treaty Organization began specifically when the Prime Minister, Calvo Sotelo, decreed in 1982 that Spain was to join. At the time the *PSOE* was moderately against the idea. In the southern Basque Country there were many demonstrations against NATO which were put down with the usual police brutality.

Towards the end of 1985 an umbrella movement was formed under the title *Manifiesto por la Soberania Nacional del Pais Vasco contra la OTAN* (Manifesto for the National Sovereignty of the Basque Country against NATO), and it was this which ensured the coherence and continuity of the campaign. The movement's name was taken from a document signed by people of various political persuasions, from which we shall quote the first and last paragraphs: 'We are against NATO because the Spanish State's continuing membership of this Alliance implies more direct intervention by the Unites States in the affairs of the Basque people, which will have political, economic, legal, military and diplomatic consequences that will no doubt aggravate the conditions under which we are struggling for our legitimate national rights.

'From this Nationalist and anti-imperialist perspective, we present this Manifesto to the Basque people, calling upon all citizens to show their support for it as proof of their resolute rejection of NATO, and we express solidarity with all other groups which have taken up their positions in the struggle, both within the Spanish State and elsewhere, against the military, repressive and imperialist objectives of NATO.'

The Manifesto movement has organized a great number of meetings in the villages of the southern Basque Country, even in the smallest of them, as well as public events of all kinds, including festivals and demonstrations in the streets of all the main centres.

The Socialist Government under Felipe González held a referendum on 12 March 1986 on the Spanish State's membership of NATO. After a highly misleading campaign, it asked — in an incredibly obtuse way — the following question: 'The Spanish Government considers that it is in the national interest that Spain should remain within the Atlantic Alliance and has decided that its membership should be ensured under the following terms:1.Spain's participation in the Atlantic Alliance shall not include its incorporation in the integrated military structure. 2. The ban on installing, stocking or introducing nuclear arms on Spanish territory will be upheld. 3. The military presence of the United States in Spain will be gradually reduced.Question: Do you think it is in Spain's interests to remain within the Atlantic Alliance under the terms agreed by the Government of the Nation?'

Out of the 29 million people whose names appeared on the electoral registers of the Spanish State, 12 million abstained (41%). The remaining 17 million cast their votes in the following ways: 9 million voted 'yes', 7 million voted 'no' and 1 million spoiled their voting papers. The Government's proposal, though oddly formulated, was clear enough, and it was therefore carried. On the other hand, in view of the uncertain response in the run-up to the referendum and its feeble outcome, the *PSOE* never again dared to consult the people by means of a referendum.

In the southern Basque Country, out of 2 million voters some 700,000 (35%) abstained, 830,000 voted 'no', 430,000 voted 'yes' and 40,000 spoiled their voting papers. The 'no' vote was therefore in a clear majority (two out of three votes) in each of the four provinces.In theory, the *PNV* allowed its supporters to cast their votes as they wished, but although publicly the party's leaders were in favour of a 'yes', the results proved that the greater part of the membership had voted 'no'. The 'no' vote was advocated by several left-wing Basque parties, in particular *Herri Batasuna*.

There are various explanations for the Basque 'no' to NATO: 1 The protection of Basque national sovereignty and a rejection of foreign interference. The direct correlation, village by village and district by district, between the 'no' vote and a knowledge of the Basque language, and between the 'no' vote and political awareness, was proof of this. The direct relationship between the rejection of NATO and its own language was also to be seen in Catalonia, which — with the Basque Country and the Canary Islands — was among those parts of the Spanish State where the degree of rejection was highly significant. 2 Linked with the foregoing explanation, the North American presence in NATO was seen, at the time, as something that belonged to the Franco regime and to a reactionary, centralist society. 3 Some commentators partly explained the 'no' vote as a protest against the anti-Basque policies of the *PSOE*.

Another feature of the Basque 'no' vote which is worth noting is the unanimity of the southern Basque Country: not only were the four provinces inclined to vote 'no', but what is more, none of the adjacent provinces chose to vote this way. This was evidence of the political unity that the Spanish Government denies in separating Navarra from its three sister-provinces.

The explanation of the Basque 'no' to NATO is therefore a fairly simple matter when the various sociological factors which define Basque society are borne in mind. On the other hand, those who have a highly idealistic view of the Basques, such as the writer Julio Caro Baroja, an expert in Basque anthropology, find it hard to understand. After the result of the referendum had been announced, he commented: 'I have given up trying to understand the way in which the people of this country think, because I am no longer able. Given the enormous number of conservative elements in the country's make-up, I cannot understand this negative attitude to NATO.'

Participatory democracy

Among the various movements worthy of consideration under this heading are the large demonstrations in favour of independence in which many Municipal Councillors have taken part side by side with members of the public; the campaign for a motor-way between Navarra and Guipúzcoa which will not have detrimental effects on the environment (this was achieved when a route was agreed between the two sides involved in the controversy); and the movement which campaigns against compulsory military service, which is highly unpopular in the Basque Country. We should also note a number of other movements, such as those working for the preservation of the environment, solidarity with other peoples and equality of the sexes, and against racism and war, as well as neighbourhood associations, self-help groups for the unemployed, facilities for young people, and so on. Other experiments of a more local kind could be added to this list. For example, there have been protests in Navarra against the rubbish-tips of Aranguren and the dam at Itoiz. Most of these demonstrations attract thousands of people. Also notable is the action of workers against the dismantling of industry and in favour of a proper economic plan for the Basque Country. But without going into further detail, we think that enough has been said to sketch in this important characteristic of the Basques.

All these initiatives, some of long standing and others of more recent date, give an over-view of an extraordinarily active, communally aware people who are full of socio-political plans for their country and who are out to solve their own problems. A people with such characteristics cannot allow itself to be incorporated within a political system that is merely representative, one in which, once the voting-papers have been dropped into the ballot-boxes, all subsequent participation is refused and no acknowledgement made of non-governmental groups — no discussion, no consultation, no explanations.

European Governments are supposed to be representative of their societies, but by linking democracy with elections in restrictive ways, they tend to consider the citizen not as a person with legal rights but more and more as a servant of the State. Governments take the view that the people's sovereignty has somehow been delegated to politicians and whenever a citizen tries to exercise his rights, they consider it to be an assault on the system and its representatives. True, it is difficult to find formulas for making connections between the governmental and the non-governmental, precisely because the introduction of this kind of democracy is of recent date and needs to be thought out in more detail. If democracy aspires to carry out the wishes of the people, it is no good providing the same model for all peoples, for they are different the one from the other. If the wish is to act democratically, the formula must be adapted in each and every case.

We have seen in earlier chapters that the Basque Country is deeply dissatisfied with both its lack of territorial unity and the inferior status of its language. It is also frustrated by the lack of a more participatory democracy. The ballot-box works but the means of connecting the various groups and associations with the country's institutional life, once the elections are over, are not functioning. There is a serious structural fault in the democracy that exists at present and if we do not understand it, it will be impossible to appreciate the frequent explosions of discontent and outbursts of radical protest which rock the Basque Country from time to time.

Political parties are machines built on a grand scale and they are usually out of touch with or not particularly sensitive to how people feel. They have a tendency to become mere electoral machines. This leads to a flaw in the relationship between institutional life and the political sensibility of the people, a tendency which is becoming more and more evident in the whole of Europe. The consequences of all this are abstention at election times, a diminution of public interest in communal matters, estrangement between politicians and citizens, and finally, a breakdown of the system itself. The baneful effects of the plethora of political parties are in fact a symptom of the present failure of representative democracy. 'Society is much richer than political parties which, moreover, do not sufficiently reflect society's interests,' said the President of Navarra, Juan Cruz Alli, on 21 September 1991.

In recent years the delegation of powers has become more indistinct, especially at the top of the major parties, which are coming to resemble one another more and more, and to decide less and less how society — including Parliaments — should be improved. The main tendency is towards authoritarianism, submission to economic oligarchies, and to other élitist powers as they exist at present. In the Basque Country, given the collective way of life on which we have already commented, it should be quite possible to put foward a more authentically indigenous model of democracy, one closer to the spirit of the people who are to be governed, one that shows more respect for each group, each valley, each town — in short, a form of democracy that is much more participatory.

Since time immemorial, there has existed among the customs of this country a degree of participation by the people in their native institutions which is as direct as that found in Switzerland, another mountainous country. Its tradition is that the upper echelons of government should not take decisions on matters which, to the detriment of no one, can be settled lower down, at a local level. There are of course some decisions which, for collective reasons, have to be taken at the highest level and a long way from the reality of daily life, particularly in a modern industrial society, but this way is at present more the rule than the exception, and here we come face to face with a major failing of the system itself.

When it was noted in Chapter 3 that, beginning during the 1960s, the Basque Nationalist Movement became more progressive, it was in reference to this aspect of political life — the constant public pressure to devise a less formal and more real kind of democracy in which the concepts of freedom, equality, respect for nature, and so on, are not only inscribed on the facades of institutions but also to be seen in the way they work. It would be difficult to deal with the various problems from which the Basque Country suffers in piece-meal fashion. For example, a sudden increase in the use of Basque is unimaginable without first solving the present dichotomy between institutions, on the one hand, and those groups which are working for the language on the other. Nor can we foresee a greater unity between the various Basque territories which does not go hand in hand with a greater participation by all the various groups which actually shape the life of the country. Nor is it easy to imagine a greater degree of democratization that does not satisfy immediately the people's desire to protect the Basque language or their country's territorial integrity.

The Basque Country has never been asked whether it wants to be a monarchy or a republic, whether it wants to be incorporated into neighbouring States, whether it prefers the Statutes in place at present in the *CAV* and Navarra or some other arrangement that offers a greater degree of sovereignty or better cohesion as a national unit. The Basques' rejection of the Spanish Constitution has been ignored, and no Spanish party nowadays dares tinker with it, for fear of Basque demands. Nor has the slightest attention been paid to the Basques' desire to stay outside NATO. All these basic questions can easily be avoided by the central powers, but no one should then deplore the protest movement that such intransigence causes.

At the referendum of October 1979, the question about the Statute of Autonomy was asked in only three of the four provinces of the southern Basque Country, which means that it had already been decided. The fact that only one question was put, which everyone knew was going to upset a large part of the population, and that the autonomy of Navarra was not to be included in the referendum, was further proof that everything had been cut and dried in advance. When options are proposed on which decisions have already been taken, the protest that follows can easily be understood. As for the acceptance of the Statute that was to be later put into effect as the *CAV*, the 53.1% of votes in favour were exaggerated, as if they compared with the 84% obtained during the time of the Republic. The comparison of these two percentages is valid as far as their form is concerned but not in their substance. In view of the complex and contradictory realities of the situation, the intelligent thing to do is to consider the form relative and not give it an absolute value.

To have imposed a single constituency for the whole of the Spanish State for the purposes of the elections to the European Parliament was not common sense. It seemed more like a lack of respect for the various parts that make up the Spanish State, and the list of examples of similar measures that have been imposed by Madrid, all legal but anti-democratic in spirit, is a long one. Early in 1992, in order to prevent an Islamic victory, the Algerian Army banned the second round of elections, in the hope that ' the tide of protest could be stopped without further consequences. Time has shown that this was a mistake,' read the editorial in *El País* on 15 February 1994. It may be an example from another country, but this is a good illustration of the fact that only to some degree can a people's will be ignored.

It may be that what is sometimes called 'the Basque question' does not seem a very pressing one, but it will not always be so. Without the slightest doubt, it will always exist as a latent problem for as long as it remains unresolved. It can be postponed for a while and the people's wishes ignored, but not indefinitely, because the people are not going to go away and the reality of their situation is permanent.

The Basques can be suppressed by the police and in fact they are. As a general rule, the only response they get is from the police. The people, and particularly the most discontented and active among them, become the real enemies of their country's institutions, its internal enemies. Whenever a false solution is applied, there is always a high price to be paid. If the problems are to be faced in a resolute way, the country's institutions will have to abandon their present abstruse way of operating. It is after all legitimate that the majority should decide a country's destiny, but it is not legitimate that the leaders of the majority parties should transform the Government into a dictatorship as far as minorities are concerned.

In the interests of democratic behaviour and efficiency in the short term, the Government and its agencies should listen to all groups: the trades unions, the non-governmental associations of all kinds which have a certain social base, and especially so when they represent socially deprived or marginalized sectors of the population.

Today it has become necessary to decide that minorities must be heard, and that their views should be represented institutionally. Permanent consultative bodies need to be established so that the authorities are able to exchange views with the various representatives of public opinion. They should also take into more careful account what is said to them and listen to constructive criticism, encouraging a more just way of doing things and co-operation at all levels. It may be that a new consultative chamber should be created, with this as its only function.

There are always many people who do not take any part in politics other than to cast their vote — and some do not even vote — because they are more or less content to leave such matters completely in the hands of the political parties. What we are proposing here is not meant to oblige these people to show interest in something with which they do not wish to be concerned. It is more a question of opening up ways for participation by those who do want it. There are in every country, and certainly in the case of the Basques, a great number of people who are able to take an active interest in collective problems in general or simply in a particular collective problem.

As a general way of proceeding, a more receptive, consultative and participatory way of holding dialogue, within a more open-minded and freer Basque society, ought to be expected not only of public bodies but also of private ones, including commercial companies, in which the point of view of the workers should be officially heard. A more real democracy in the working of institutions goes hand in hand with a more real democracy in the running of private enterprises. Another way specially designed for closing the gap between institutions and the daily life of the people is the use of the referendum. It often happens that voters choose a party to run the country while at the same time being opposed to some aspects of its programme. The voter's identification with a party does not always imply support for all its aims.

Italy, which during the 1960s voted the Christian Democrats into power, a party opposed to divorce, voted at about the same time in favour of divorce in a famous referendum. In the same way, at the time of the Spanish Government's referendum on membership of NATO, given that the two majority parties in the Basque Country were in favour of a 'yes' vote, one might have expected the electoral response to have been in the affirmative also. But, on the contrary, it turned out to be clearly in the negative. These apparent contradictions are inexplicable only for those who simplify reality, attributing to life a linear rationality which it usually does not have, or those who prefer to think in absolute rather than in relative terms. If there existed on the Government's part a wish to be democratic, to listen to the country and its point of view, the referendum would not have the wholly exceptional character that it has today, but would be used more often and with greater facility. It seems that nowadays the authorities are afraid of the referendum when they have doubts about its result and, even more (although this may seem hard to believe) when they foresee a result which runs counter to the position taken up by the ruling party.

In the Basque Country, there is need for fewer institutions, as was suggested in Chapter 1, but more unitary ones. Now we can add that there is a need for fewer elections and more referenda. The last referendum to take place in the Spanish State was the one on membership of NATO, which the Government managed to win with such great difficulty. After that, it chose not to run any more risks; for example, the Treaty of Maastricht, which in some countries was put to referendum in 1992 and 1993, in Spain was only approved by the *Cortes*. The leaders of the main parties prefer to dictate their policies, in order to extend their influence over all parts of the State, including those where they know the opinion of the majority to be against them. But only in the short term. Such considerations, which unfortunately apply these days to many countries, are particularly relevant in the case of the Basques, where the breakdown in the relationship between government and society is clearer than in any other part of Europe.

Chapter 9

A PEOPLE'S RIGHT TO
SELF-DETERMINATION

A comparison of the Basque and Irish cases

The Basque protest movement is often compared with those in other countries, sometimes with a view to finding similarities in the armed struggle or else in the Nationalist nature of the conflict. The case with which it can be best compared is probably that of Ireland, another European country, where both the armed struggle and the national element are to be found.

Ireland has about 5 million inhabitants, 70% of whom live in the Irish Republic and 30% in the six northern counties under British rule., The population of the Basque Country is approximately 2,873,000, of whom 91% live in the southern provinces under the jurisdiction of Spain and 9% in the north under that of France. Whenever a Spaniard goes to Bayonne or Biarritz, he goes into France, but when a Basque from the south makes the same journey he goes 'to the north' or 'to the other side' . The Spaniard refers to 'Spain' or 'France' whereas the Basque calls them 'the Spanish State' or 'the French State' , thus making clear (with these cumbersome expressions) his respect for the Basque point of view, since the Basques have never been consulted as to whether they want to belong to Spain and France.

A similar terminological precision is to be found in Ireland and one of the things that strikes Basques whenever they talk to Irish people is that they too have recourse to correcting certain English usages. Those who are in favour of the unification of the island call themselves Nationalists or Republicans (and sometimes Catholics) and they call their opponents Unionists, that is those who favour the union with Great Britain, or else Protestants.

For Nationalists the town known to Unionists as Londonderry is

Derry. Nationalists do not use the name Northern Ireland, nor Ulster, for the real Ulster is a much bigger region which includes three counties more than the six under British rule. They always refer to Northern Ireland as 'the six counties' and southern Ireland as 'the twenty-six counties' . For them, those whom their opponents call 'terrorists' are 'volunteers' .

There is another striking similarity between Ireland and the Basque Country: a substantial part of the population, though preferring an end to the conflict just like the rebels, by which they mean a free and united country, show no interest in the question, out of sheer fatigue after such a prolonged conflict. They get on with their daily lives and go about their business as if this problem did not exist. In both cases moderate Nationalism co-operates with the oppressor to an extent that is moderate or immoderate according to one's point of view. Similarly, in both countries, the Church — the same Catholic Church — tends to favour the oppressor rather than the rebels, and encourages submission to the oppressor with whom it largely agrees. In both Ireland and the Basque Country the majority parties attempt to deprive the rebels of a hearing, denying them access to the media and refusing to talk to them in public. The most combative section of both these peoples has become in time, somewhat in spite of itself, the repository of the Nationalist tradition, the lone defender of the ideas of national renewal that were first mooted at the end of the last century and at the beginning of this.

What is more, both *Sinn Féin* (which means 'Ourselves Alone') and *Herri Batasuna* ('Unity of the People') reject the autonomous parliaments which have been set up, considering them irrelevant to the real resolution of the conflict. In the case of Ireland, we refer to the Assembly at Stormont, which existed up to the end of the 1960s, and in that of the Basque Country, to the Parliaments in Vitoria and Pamplona, which are still in operation. A few years ago the President of *Sinn Féin*, Gerry Adams, said: 'We reject all arrangements which apply only to the six counties, whether or not they have the support of Dublin.' In the same way, *Herri Batasuna* refuses to accept decisions relating only to the southern provinces of the Basque Country.

The fact that both these causes rely in part on the use of arms creates, moreover, a social momentum that is similar in both cases. One product of these is the movement for the aid of political prisoners and the denunciation of police torture. Both situations and organizations create social micro-climates which resemble each other.

Both conflicts have to do with the presence of a frontier which separates the two countries, although in a different way, north from south, and which has made the armed struggle easier, at least to some extent and up to recent times.

The section of the population which is involved in the conflict is probably also the most creative and lively, despite the fact that it is somewhat turned in on itself, cut off in a small world of its own, a little out of touch with the triviality that surrounds it. The relationship between *Sinn Féin* and the Irish Republican Army is probably similar to that between *Herri Batasuna* and *ETA*, and although we are in no position to deny or confirm it, this comparison is often made.

A comparison between the linguistic situation in each of these countries, which have more similarities than differences, would require separate treatment. The fortunes of the Basque language have been described in Chapter 2. As for Ireland, which has a population of 5 million north and south, only about 35,000 people use the Irish language (a Celtic language very different from English) on a daily basis. They live in small villages scattered in several districts in the westernmost extremities of the island. It appears that between about 100,000 and 200,000 others are able to speak the language to some extent. These small districts where Irish is usually spoken are known as the *Gaeltacht* and, in the Republic, the Government has a special (but very inadequate) policy for the maintenance of their monolingual character. Although the Government's commitment is very feeble, at least it has one advantage in that the law allows the implementation of this policy in the Irish-speaking areas. In the case of Basque a similar policy would not be allowed by law. In the Spanish State, as was shown in Chapter 2, the Spanish language is compulsory for the whole population and the only compulsory language, and the same is true in the French State of the French language.

Although a theoretical knowledge of Irish has been maintained in recent years by about 6% of the Republic's population, its practical use (which has always been weak) has decreased to an extraordinary degree. Nevertheless, the public's moral support for the language is well defined. At every opinion poll the public appear to be enthusiastic on this score. There are then certain resemblances between the situations of Irish and Basque: a level of understanding which is not inconsiderable and which goes hand in hand with weak use of the language and yet very strong public support.

Although in the Irish Republic the language is compulsory in education, the need to know it in order to obtain the primary school certificate and to fill posts that used to require it, was done away with several years ago. Since the beginning of the 1970s there have been schools which teach through the medium of Irish. Whereas in the north they are few in number and private, in the Republic there are a lot of them and they are public. This phenomenon has proceeded apace in recent years, supported mainly by working-class people. These schools used to draw on the support of the middle-classes, who wanted to help their children find jobs, but now that this incentive no longer exists, the motivation for the creation of these schools has become more Nationalist in character.

Adopting terminology used in Chapter 2, we could say that the Irish Government has developed, with regard to the native language, a policy of 'diffusion' (support for the language in education and the media) as well as a 'territorial' policy (support for monolingualism in the *Gaeltacht*), albeit very weak support in both instances, so that Irish seems to be on the point of disappearing as a living language.

The lower classes have played only a limited role in leading the independence movement in the south of Ireland. But this section of the population, which has a very acute awareness of the question, is also the most favourably disposed towards the use of Irish. This has led, among other negative consequences, to a rather lopsided form of independence as far as the language is concerned. The legal status of Irish is superior to that of Welsh or Basque, but its real strength is clearly inferior.

Among other possibilities, it is quite feasible to imagine a similar scenario for the Basque Country, with the disappearance of the language, in which the two main strands of the Nationalist movement — the more moderate and the more radical — do not co-operate in advancing towards sovereignty. Because moderate Nationalism is based on a consensus agreed with Madrid, its proponents are under an obligation (whether they like it or not) to politicize their linguistic policies, to impose conditions formulated by political parties, to prefer the stagnation of the Basque language rather than to show publicly to Madrid, on this question as on any other, that it is a friend of 'terrorists'. This is a disastrous decision for the future of the language.

The language question allows us to draw some comparisons between the Basque case and the Irish, and to point to some of the differences that exist between them. For the Irish, the main objective of their struggle is the reunification of their country, whereas for the Basques the principal aim is to claim their right to self-determination, with a view to protecting their national identity, mainly by saving their language. It is clear that, for the Basques, territorial reunification is a matter of fundamental importance, just as it is for the Koreans, and as it used to be for the Germans or the Vietnamese.

But in this context, the immediate objective is more the reunification of the four southern provinces than, at least for the moment, the reunification of the north with the south. For the Irish, though, north-south reunification is the key-question. On the other hand, the Irish believe their language to be lost, or at least they behave as if they consider it lost. The language certainly figures among their national objectives, but it does not seem to carry much weight in the reality of their struggle. Among the Basques, however, public support for the *ikastola*, for the schools in which adults are taught to read and write the language, for those districts which live and work in Basque, for the Basque-language media and the appointment of Basque-speaking civil servants, is constant. The risk that the language might disappear is the greatest worry agitating the Basques, for it is the mirror in which their gradual effacement as a people is reflected.

There are other signs of the Basque identity, for example in the cultural, sporting, gastronomical and festive fields. But the language is at the heart of all these and traditionally it has been the very symbol of Basque identity. The real strength of the Basque language is much superior to that of Irish and the importance attributed to it is also much greater. There may be a relationship based on cause and effect between these two questions, between the language's strength and the role it plays in the protest movement. The Irish language's close proximity to death may not explain the Irish movement, but nevertheless, these two factors are closely intertwined.

In the Basque case, the linguistic argument is quite simply a key question, although public awareness of this phenomenon is somewhat inconsistent. If, however, the question is considered in terms of the collective subconscious, it explains perfectly well the Basque protests (and perhaps something similar happened in Ireland at the beginning of the century), although some Basques, even many Basques, seem not to consider the language important or believe they do not. The loss of the Basque language goes hand in hand with the loss of collective identity and the death-throes through which it has been going during the course of the 20th century creates among Basques an acutely existential anguish, which is more or less conscious and capable of engendering great violence. There are serious reasons for thinking that a vigorous plan for linguistic recovery throughout the Basque Country, with clear and tangible results, could put an end to the more extreme forms of protest. If the Basque language were to be perceived as having an assured future, the people's grievances would be expressed in other ways. If to that were added some form of institutional recognition of Basque territorial unity, the perspective would be utterly transformed. Sovereignty — by which is meant an advanced Statute for the four southern provinces and a Basque *département* in the north — together with the right to self-determination, are doubtless what the Basques want, but in the collective subconscious the primary objective is to ensure the language's survival and the second is territorial unity.

There are, however, other differences between the two national causes that we have been comparing. The armed struggle in Ireland has clearly been stronger than that in the Basque Country, as is shown by the number of incidents and victims, as well as by the presence of the British Army in the streets of the north. *Sinn Féin* has received a good deal of support from people of Irish extraction in America who still have strongly Nationalist feelings about Ireland, whereas people of Basque background living in the United States, although they may be Nationalist in sympathy, seem to be content with the present set-up in the southern provinces and most of them do not support *ETA*.

But the fundamental difference between the two cases is that, in the north of Ireland, two communities are in confrontion with each other, which is not the case in the Basque Country. In what is called Ulster a very large part of the population is pro-British and express themselves accordingly against those on the other side. This is to be seen not only at election time but also in street-demonstrations and in clandestine operations against Republicans. Two thirds of the population are Protestant and most of them are pro-British, while the other third are Catholic and pro-Irish. Industry and services are in Protestant hands, whereas agriculture is practised mainly by Catholics who suffer discrimination when it comes to employment and subsidized housing.

At the present time it appears that there are more difficulties in solving the Irish problem within the pro-British section of the population in northern Ireland than there are among the people of Britain itself, who seem more inclined to abandon their interests there in order to avoid further problems. (It could also be argued that the population of the Republic would be prepared to leave the north in British hands, and for the same reason.) The difficulty in reaching a political solution in Ireland lies in the confrontation between the two communities, or more precisely, in the intransigence of the pro-British majority when it comes to the question of reuniting the island. The problem was created by the British at the time of partition, but it now has a momentum of its own.

In the Basque case, the population as a whole is largely Nationalist in sympathy, or at least it gives its backing to Nationalist aims.

It does so in a somewhat cautious way and in direct proportion to the degree of Nationalist conviction. Militant patriotism of the Spanish or French kind, and irritation at Basque grievances, do not come naturally to the Basques but are brought in from outside. Although there are isolated instances of anti-Basque feeling, we cannot speak of two communities in confrontation with each other, whereas in the north of Ireland that is very much the case. This is essentially why, in fact, the solution of the Basque problem is vastly less complicated than that of the Irish, if only we could set aside all those broken promises.

Nevertheless, the recent history of the two conflicts suggests that greater progress towards a negotiated settlement is being made in Ireland than in the Basque Country. Let us look quickly at the chronology of Irish freedom.

The Irish Republican Brotherhood, founded in 1858, took as its aim the awakening of Ireland's patriotic conscience. Twelve years later there was a new movement claiming the right to Irish self-government. In 1902 *Sinn Féin* was founded, a para-military movement calling for Irish independence. In 1914, the year in which the First World War broke out, the Protestant minority in Ulster tried to put off the granting of Irish self-government which had recently been approved, and which was eventually accepted, although the war would defer its implementation. In 1916, in the middle of world war, Irish Nationalists organized in Dublin the famous Easter Rising against British rule in Ireland This brought a furious response from the British who executed its leaders, thus causing anti-British feeling throughout the island. Two years later, in 1918, *Sinn Féin* won a massive electoral victory, after which the elected M.Ps. decided not to take their seats at Westminster but to form an Irish Assembly.

The British attempt to crush *Sinn Féin* led to the Anglo-Irish War of 1919-21, which ended when independence was granted to 26 of the 32 counties within the context of the British Commonwealth, the other six counties remaining under British rule. Thus the British succeeded in transforming the Protestant minority into a majority in the north of Ireland, in a region defined in an arbitrary manner, which would remain in their hands. From 1921 to 1923 there was a civil war in the south between those who were opposed to partition and those who accepted it, the latter winning.

In 1937 Ireland declared itself a sovereign State to be known as *Eire*, which is the island's name in Irish. After the Second World War, during which Ireland remained neutral, the south declared itself a Republic in 1949 and left the British Commonwealth, maintaining its Constitution of 1937. Ireland joined the United Nations in 1955.

Since winning independence the Irish Republic has been governed alternately by *Fine Gael* (the heirs of those who accepted partition) and *Fianna Fail* (the heirs of those who were opposed to partition), the latter being in power in 1994. In 1973 the Republic joined the European Economic Community.

Since 1969 the movement in favour of the incorporation of the six northern counties into the Republic has made a comeback under the instigation of its armed wing, the IRA, and its political wing, *Sinn Féin*, which operates in both parts of the island, north and south. The British Army, which scorns and hates the Irish, now occupies the six counties, reinforcing the role of the Royal Ulster Constabulary. More than 3,000 people have been killed in the conflict since 1969.

In 1985 *Sinn Féin* put up candidates in the municipal elections in the north and they took the seats to which they had been elected. Usually the party wins about 10% of the votes in the north, where it is the fourth largest party in electoral terms, and a much lower percentage in the south.

At the end of 1985 the Irish Government came to an agreement with the Conservative Government of Margaret Thatcher that was known as the Hillsborough Accord, by which it acquired a new right to have its say on British policy in the north in exchange for acknowledging Britain's right to run the six counties, also agreeing to take more stringent measures against Irish Nationalism there.

On 24 April 1993, in the biggest operation ever undertaken by the IRA, a series of large explosions destroyed a large part of the City of London, the heart of the British financial empire. In the following autumn, the two northern Irish parties representing Catholics, *Sinn Féin* and the Social Democratic Labour Party, signed an agreement, for the very first time, with a view to starting a process of negotiation between all the parties involved. The latter, known by its initials SDLP, is the more moderate of the two and is opposed to the armed struggle. This bi-partite accord marked an important milestone in Irish history and had a very powerful impact on public opinion in both parts of the island.

At the end of 1993, it was confirmed that there had been secret contacts between the IRA and the British Government. On 15 December the famous Downing Street Declaration was signed, under which the Prime Minister of Great Britain, the Conservative John Major, and the Prime Minister of Ireland, Albert Reynolds, acknowledged that Ireland, under certain conditions, had the right to self-determination and reunification. *Sinn Féin* responded to this declaration by expressing, on the one hand, its satisfaction while, on the other, asking for a series of clarifications. The clarifications requested amounted to an assurance that the British Government really did recognize the Irish people's rights in these two respects. It is not known whether the caution shown by *Sinn Féin* in its desire to have assurances about the British will to negotiate before the party agreed to enter into negotiations had been learned from the talks in Algiers between the Spanish Government and *ETA*, but there is reason for believing so. The breaking off of these latter talks, and the Madrid Government's failure to honour the agreements reached by its own delegates in Algiers, had revealed a basic lack of will to negotiate on the part of the Spanish Government. Since then *ETA* has continued to make it clear that before taking part in further talks it would have to be given assurances that the Spanish side really is ready for dialogue. The cautious response by *Sinn Féin* to the Downing Street Declaration appears to take account of this lesson from recent Basque history.

However, that does not mean that *Sinn Féin* has under-estimated the importance of the Declaration. Gerry Adams, the Party's President, during a visit to the Basque Country at the invitation of *Herri Batasuna*, wrote as follows: 'We accept completely the idea that in working towards peace, there will be no quick solutions or agreements. The peace progress has been set in motion and our immediate task is to take it forward. The Downing Street Declaration of last December is a stage in the slow and painful process of separating Great Britain from its first and last colony. I am convinced that we are living through the final phase of the Anglo-Irish conflict.' In January and February of the same year, Gerry Adams managed to arrange for the first time a visit to the United States, once the ban on his visa had been lifted. This trip allowed him to make direct contact with the Irish diaspora, who are broadly in favour of the reunification of Ireland, and to explain his point of view to the American public.

At the end of June, the British Government announced that a large number of Irish political prisoners in British gaols would be transferred to prisons in the north of Ireland, thus conceding a long-standing claim, the aim of which was humanitarian — to facilitate visits by the prisoners' families. In Ireland, as in the Basque Country, prisoners' families have been obliged to make long and expensive journeys, often to find that their relatives had been transferred to another prison, without their having been informed of it in advance. The IRA ceasefire of September 1994 and events subsequent to it marked the beginning of political talks between Britain and Ireland, with the aim of transforming the armed conflict into peaceful negotiation. All this came about after and, arguably, mainly as a result of the bombing of the City of London in April 1993. A fresh round of talks scheduled for May-June 1996, from which *Sinn Féin* was excluded, coincided with another huge explosion in England, this time in the heart of Manchester, for which the IRA claimed responsibility.

New States in Europe

The division of the world into the existing Nation-States has long seemed to be set in concrete, something that could seldom if ever be modified and never on our own patch. This assumption was very general in Europe after the Second World War and up to the 1990s. But then it broke down. Indeed, frontiers are more changeable than they seem and more open to discussion than we thought. Throughout the world there has been a slow but uninterrupted redrawing of frontiers.

To begin with the Spanish State, about 50 territories have broken away since the beginning of its empire, from the end of the 15th century to our own times, from the Netherlands in 1579 to Cuba, the Phillipines and Puerto Rico in 1898, as well as many colonies in Italy, the Near East and the Americas. As for the 20th century, after the Second World War, Northern Morocco seceded in 1956, Equatorial Guinea and Ifni in 1969 and the Sahara in 1975.

In, addition to those which broke away from the Spanish State, about a hundred countries have obtained their independence throughout the world, quite a few of them former colonies of France. In Europe the following countries have gained their freedom:

    1905 Norway (from Sweden)
    1917 Finland (from Russia)
    1918 Iceland (from Denmark)
    1918 Czechoslovakia, Hungary and Poland
         (from Austria-Hungary)
    1949 The Republic of Ireland (from Great Britain)
    1960 Cyprus (from Great Britain)
    1964 Malta (from Great Britain)

But the real commotion has been caused by the appearance of new European States emerging from the old Union of Socialist Soviet Republics, Czechoslovakia and Yugoslavia, after the dismantling of the Berlin Wall in 1989, which in turn paved the way for the reunification of Germany; here is a list of them:

    1991 Armenia
    1991 Azerbaijan

1991 Belorussia
1991 Croatia
1991 Slovenia
1991 Estonia
1991 Georgia
1991 Lithuania
1991 Macedonia
1991 Moldavia
1991 Russia
1991 The Ukraine
1992 Bosnia Hercegovinia
1992 Serbia and Montenegro
1993 Slovakia
1993 The Czech Republic

The right of self-determination

The Basque tradition, although upheld in various ways over the centuries, has always been based on respect for the country's usages and customs, for its own legal system, within the framework of the foral laws which survived up to the Carlist Wars. It is to these we refer when we speak of the historical rights of the Basque Country. However, no one these days is asking for the re-establishment of such ancient laws, which are anyway not appropriate to the modern world. Although Basque demands, as always, are today still rooted in the fostering of the national identity and respect for the will of the people, their modern expression takes the form of a demand for self-determination, which means simply that the people have the right to decide their own future. This is the inherent right of every people to choose its own fate, whether it be integration with other peoples or separate statehood.

This collective right was postulated and formulated during the French Revolution of 1789 and the concept continued to be developed during the 19th century, but it received a new and powerful lease of life with the spread of Leninism during the first part of the 20th century. If life, freedom and work are basic human rights, the right to self-determination is also a fundamental right for peoples, and might even be a condition of their very existence. Nothing justifies its suppression or its limitation, neither among peoples with their own States nor among those which form part of multi-national States.' This right,' the President of *Sinn Féin* wrote during his visit to the Basque Country, 'also prevents the breaking up of a nation's unity or territorial integrity. The partition of Ireland deprives the right of the Irish people to self-determination.'

The USA has been the main champion of the right to self-determination. After the First World War it took a great interest in the dismemberment of the German Empire and, after 1945, in the decolonization policies of Great Britain and France. During the 1990s, the emergence of new States from the former USSR, which had also helped to define this right, at least in theory, was also of interest to the Americans. The words of President George Bush illustrate the American way of thinking during this latter phase. Towards the end of May 1990, he excused his very cautious support for the Soviet President, Gorbachov, thus: 'Every American President will find it difficult to offer you help for as long as self-determination is not on offer for the Baltic countries.'

Inasmuch as it is a right of all peoples, the right to self-determination predates the State and does not depend on any acknowledgement from that quarter. Most States have preferred to view this right in political rather than in legal terms, more pragmatically than as a matter of principle, in order not to have to redraw their internal borders. However, it is a legal principle which is based on concepts of democracy and liberty. It is these, together with the historical characteristics making up an ethnic group, which transform the natural community into a political one. They proclaim its existence, determining the boundaries of the people's territory and deciding its political relations with others. Certain international agreements recognize and subscribe to this principle. The Charter of the United Nations (1945) opens by defining among its objectives 'the development of friendly relations between nations, founded on respect for the principle of equal rights of the peoples and their right to decide their own destinies.' The International Accords on Human Rights of 16 December 1966 (Civil and Political Rights and Economic, Social and Cultural Rights) which were ratified by the Spanish and French States, include the words: 'All peoples have the right to self-determination. By virtue of this right, they are able freely to determine their economic life and provide for their economic, social and cultural development.' The Helsinki Declaration of 1975 includes in the 8th clause of its final version the right of peoples to self-determination and sets out criteria for mutual relations between States. The Algiers Charter, also known as the Universal Declaration on the Rights of Peoples (4 July 1976) states in Article 5: 'Every people has an uncircumscribable and inalienable right to self-determination. This right determines its political status in complete freedom and without any interference from outside.'

Lawyers in all parts of the world argue as to whether these declarations should apply only to colonies or whether they may also be applied to national minorities which exist inside States, such as the Basques. The same European States which refuse the right of self-determination to territories incorporated within their borders, such as Corsica, Catalonia, Scotland, Wales, Brittany, South Tyrol or the Basque Country, in recent years have approved and even supported the self-determination of Croatia, Slovakia, Lithuania and so many other countries which were once part of Communist States. These countries, too, are European, and they were once incorporated in larger States. They also have on their territories fairly large minorities belonging to the dominant ethnic groups. Yet by winning their independence they have demonstrated that self-determination is not a right that is reserved for other continents but that Europe accepts it and that the principle is at the very heart of the new Europe. It was precisely the right of self-determination that was invoked by Governments and by the media at the time of German reunification. But the unity of the two parts of the Basque Country remains illegal.

As far as the Basque case is concerned, lawyers who put Spanish nationality before Basque nationality lend their support to the view that the right of self-determination applies only to colonies in the Third World and that, as a consequence, States which refuse this right to ethnic groups living on their territories cannot be accused of being undemocratic. They also claim that in the Basque case it is not clear to whom this right belongs, that General Elections are already an exercise in self-determination, that in a democratic State only individual self-determination and not the collective kind makes any sense, and so on. These lawyers also saw an exercise in self-determination in the referendum on the Statute of the Basque Autonomous Community (*CAV*) in 1979, despite the fact that Navarra was not included in that exercise. However, this Statute is not recognized by the Basque people. Its text was substantially altered in Madrid and what is more, it allows only for administrative decentralization with no political clout and rejects the other possibilities that go with the right of self-determination that have been clearly demanded by the Basque people. It is a mistake to see in this referendum an exercise in self-determination. Nor can it be argued that this Statute provides a means for the subsequent development of the right to self-determination, for it refuses both the sovereignty of the Basque people and its territorial integrity; it is, moreover, subordinate to a Constitution that does not allow self-determination. On the contrary, this Statute was merely a way of muzzling the Basque people and preventing it from gaining its sovereignty.

The words of a Basque leader of the *Alianza Popular* (Popular Alliance), a right-wing Spanish party, which was a forerunner of the present-day *Partido Popular* (Popular Party), confirm this last point. The *Alianza Popular* was officially opposed to the Statute during the referendum of 1979, although it was known to have advised its supporters to vote in favour. In any case, a short while after the referendum, Julien Guimon, one of the party's leaders, stated: 'Today the *Alianza Popular* gives its complete approval to the Basque Statute as a more effective way of protecting the unity of all Spaniards.' Furthermore, those who argue that the Basque people is deprived — whether morally or by existing laws — of the right to self-determination, contradict themselves when they say that the Basques won this right at the time of the referendum or that they exercise it regularly during the course of the other elections. Expression of the people's will becomes redundant if the right to self-determination has not been granted, and so the Basque people have not exercised it.

Contrary to the pronouncements of the lawyers whom we have just quoted, those who respect Basque nationality, be they Basques or not, consider that the clauses of the various international agreements recognize the right of self-determination not only for colonies but also for peoples incorporated in States, for otherwise they would be limited to recognizing only constituted States and to confirming the restrictions which already exist within their borders. Furthermore, the Declarations on Human Rights of 1966 would not have spoken specifically of 'all peoples' but would have confined this general formula to 'all States' or 'colonized peoples' if that had been the intention. The United Nations Organization has recognized the self-determination of Palestine and the Sahara, which are two peoples with no State of their own.

This second group of lawyers take the view that the degree of democracy within a State can be measured by how much self-management it allows its constituent parts, at all levels, both individual and collective. But the very fact there is discussion on the various interpretations of these clauses means, on the one hand, that they have not been fully implemented, for they have an ambiguity on which an incontestable right cannot be based, and on the other, that their application in such cases as the Basque has not been clearly rejected either.

Nearer in time and space, we might point to the celebration of the *Aberri Eguna* (the national day) on 27 March 1978. Demonstrators carried banners calling for Basque self-determination, and among them were several leaders of the *PSOE*. All this was going on at a time when the text of the State Constitution was being concocted in Madrid. The communiqué drawn up on that occasion by all political parties taking part in the celebration, except for those on the Spanish Right, read as follows: 'The obtaining of a National Statute of Autonomy for Navarra, Álava, Guipúzcoa and Vizcaya is an urgent necessity which we demand as the indispensable condition for normalization in the political life of *Euskadi.* Democracy for our people will not be complete, in constitutional terms, unless there is recognition of its sovereignty and the right to govern itself which makes self-determination possible.'

But this aspiration on the part of the large majority of the Basque people — territorial unity and self-determination — was betrayed a short while afterwards. The Constitution that was in preparation at the time was implicitly opposed to recognizing the right to self-determination, despite being intended for a State that is clearly multinational, given that it includes Galicia, a part of Catalonia and a part of the Basque Country. The Statute of Autonomy that was put into effect in the year following was applied not to the four Basque provinces but to three.

The Spanish Constitution of 1978 recognizes only 'the Spanish people' and speaks only of its 'indissoluble unity', just as the French Constitution of 1958 recognizes only 'the French people'. The Basque people exists in reality but not according to the two Constitutions in force on its territory. The right to self-determination is deprived of meaning in both Constitutions. The French Constitution had to put up with the secession of Algeria which at the time consisted of only a few French *départements.* In the same way the Spanish Constitution will have to put up with the incorporation into Morocco of Ceuta and Melilla, which at present are Spanish provinces. Clause 8 of the Constitution adds that 'the mission of the armed forces is to guarantee the sovereignty and independence of Spain, to protect its territorial integrity and to oversee the implementation of the Constitution' . The second of these refers directly to the self-determination of part of the State, which means that this question is legally subordinate, whatever the prevailing conditions, to the power of the Spanish Army. Self-determination is therefore proscribed and legally subordinated to the role of violence.

On 10 July 1994 the newspaper *El País* made an assessment of the reduction in the armed forces which had just been announced by the Ministry of Defence. Some 40,000 men were to be made redundant throughout Spain except for the Basque Country and Catalonia which had been 'almost emptied ' of army personnel up to then. The four capitals of the southern Basque Country would continue to be bases for battalions and regiments, which 'will be reinforced in times of crisis by reservists and their mission will be to protect the territorial integrity of Spain'.

The Spanish Constitution was put to referendum in all parts of the State so that the majority of votes cast on this territory would be the decisive factor. Thus the recognition or non-recognition of the Basque people had been decided in advance, before the referendum had even taken place. The Constitution was therefore implemented before it was approved. The way in which the question was put determined the reply.

A majority of voters in the southern Basque Country refused to approve the Spanish Constitution of 1978, but paradoxically the people's response could not be put into operation because it had been cancelled in advance by the terms of the Constitution itself. By the same token, this rejection removed all moral force from constitutional legitimacy in the southern Basque Country, although we must remember that in the north the French Constitution was approved. The Spanish way of reasoning at the present time is, 'You do not exist, Basque Country, because the Constitution does not recognize you.' Previously it was 'As I do not recognize you, your response to the Constitution does not concern me.' The non-recognition of the Basque Country is still a point of departure, although it is sometimes presented as if it were a point of arrival.

'The *PNV* will go on rejecting the Constitution,' said the party's President, Xavier Arzalluz, on 14 February 1988, and perhaps for that reason. 'The Constitution threatens force against every people that wants to claim its rights,' he said a few years later on 29 September 1991, adding: 'The problem has existed ever since we were deprived of our sovereignty by armed force.' More recently, on 17 November 1993, Arzulluz said: 'If a people does not want to be part of a State, it is shameful to force them into it.' A few months later, on 3 June 1994, he stated: 'They have Clause 8 in the Constitution which entrusts territorial unity to the Army. Don't let them tell us that it can be protected without having recourse to violence!' In its edition of 17 July 1994, *El País* reported Arzulluz as follows: 'We are one people, one ethnic group, with one language, a distinct population which has its own identity and the right to exercise its own political power, to form a Basque State. We, the Basques, will not allow this right to be denied us, either by armed force or by any other means.'

'The violence carried out in the first instance is that done by the Spanish State,' said the Catalan Nationalist leader Angel Colom on 2 August 1991, 'for the State does not recognize the right to self-determination of the three nations incorporated within it.'

The Basque people's attachment to the right of self-determination has been demonstrated many times over by immense crowds in the streets of Pamplona, Bilbao and other towns in the southern provinces. This right is refused them in law and is difficult to promote in elections and in the media, which remain openly hostile. Those who claim the right to self-determination are deprived, in the legal and political framework which exists at present, of the means which might allow its implementation, unless it be in a gradual way, and they are calling for some other context which would make it possible. As far as the Spanish Constitution is concerned, it would not be the first time for it to be amended, because it was changed during the 1990s to take account of the Maastricht Treaty which insists that all citizens are able to stand as candidates at elections in all the countries which have signed that agreement.

The case made out, in February 1990, by the Parliament in Vitoria, legally representing the three western provinces of the Basque Country (the *CAV*) — under pressure from the Nationalist eruption in Eastern Europe — proved the impossibility of exercizing the right to self-determination for the present. On that occasion the votes of the three moderate Nationalist parties, which were in favour, were more than the votes of the Spanish parties, which were opposed. A statement was drawn up which claimed the right to Basque self-determination, but limiting it to the *CAV* and with an additional clause making it clear that the statement was purely doctrinal and not necessarily a practical scheme, and that any possible implemetation of it would have to come about within the framework of the Constitution.

But is this right really a panacea capable of solving the main problem of the Basque Country? Historical, sociological and psychological analyses, taken together, suggest that it is indeed the Gordian knot of the Basque conflict. If the country were to be granted this right, its deepest and most intimate wish — the simple desire to be recognized as a country and people — would be satisfied. If it does not recover its language and ensure a future for it, if it cannot grasp the political means of governing itself and safeguarding its identity, the Basque people — dispersed between two powerful States — runs the serious risk of disappearing as such. The fact that its right to self-determination is not recognized is a threat to its very existence. Such recognition would, moreover, have the advantage of not having any negative consequences. In winning it, the Basque Country would draw benefit from it without causing anyone harm. As for the ideological objection that might be expected from Spanish Nationalists, there is nothing that makes us think of that as a negative consequence. Another advantage would be its negligible cost in financial terms. If it is a good thing to satisfy the Basques on this score and put an end to the conflict, without a prohibitive economic sacrifice, that is surely a double merit.

In any case, whether it is recognized or not, the right to self-determination is concomitant with the recognition of equality between peoples and flows from the democratic concept that sovereignty rests with the people and is inalienable. There is no better guarantee of peace and international co-operation. On the other hand, although its democratic character may be difficult to put into effect, the right to self-determination will not come about unless there is some political authority to sanction it, as usually happens with other elementary rights claimed by individuals or peoples.

INDEX